Bret Harte, Bret Harte

The heritage of Dedlow Marsh, and other tales

Bret Harte, Bret Harte

The heritage of Dedlow Marsh, and other tales

ISBN/EAN: 9783743303164

Manufactured in Europe, USA, Canada, Australia, Japa

Cover: Foto ©ninafisch / pixelio.de

Manufactured and distributed by brebook publishing software (www.brebook.com)

Bret Harte, Bret Harte

The heritage of Dedlow Marsh, and other tales

THE
HERITAGE OF DEDLOW MARSH

AND OTHER TALES

THE HERITAGE
OF DEDLOW MARSH

AND OTHER TALES

BY

BRET HARTE

IN TWO VOLUMES—VOL. I

London
MACMILLAN AND CO.
AND NEW YORK
1889

All rights reserved

CONTENTS

		PAGE
I. THE HERITAGE OF DEDLOW MARSH	. .	1
II. A KNIGHT-ERRANT OF THE FOOT-HILLS	.	135

I

THE
HERITAGE OF DEDLOW MARSH

THE
HERITAGE OF DEDLOW MARSH

I

THE sun was going down on the Dedlow Marshes. The tide was following it fast, as if to meet the reddening lines of sky and water in the west, leaving the foreground to grow blacker and blacker every moment, and to bring out in startling contrast the few half-filled and half-lit pools left behind, and forgotten. The strong breath of the Pacific fanning their surfaces at times kindled them into a dull glow like dying embers. A cloud of sand-pipers rose white from one of the nearer lagoons, swept in a long eddying ring against the sunset, and became a black and dropping rain to seaward. The long sinuous line of channel, fading with the light and ebbing with the tide, began to give off here and there light puffs of gray-winged birds like sudden exhalations. High in the darkening sky the long arrow-headed lines of geese and 'brant' pointed towards the upland. As the light grew more uncertain the air at times was filled with the rush of viewless and melancholy wings, or became plaintive with far-off cries and lamentations. As the Marshes grew blacker the far-scattered tussocks and accretions on its level surface began to loom in exaggerated outline, and two human figures, suddenly emerging erect on the bank of the hidden channel, assumed the proportion of giants.

When they had moored their unseen boat, they still appeared for some moments to be moving vaguely and aimlessly around the spot where they had disembarked. But as the eye became familiar with the darkness it was seen that they were really advancing inland, yet with a slowness of progression and deviousness of course that appeared inexplicable to the distant spectator. Presently it was evident that this seemingly even, vast, black expanse was traversed and intersected by inky creeks and small channels, which made human progression difficult and dangerous. As they appeared nearer, and their figures took more natural proportions, it could be seen that each carried a gun; that one was a young girl, although dressed so like her companion in shaggy pea-jacket and sou'wester as to be scarcely distinguished from him above the short skirt that came half way down her high indiarubber fishing boots. By the time they had reached firmer ground, and turned to look back at the sunset, it could be also seen that the likeness between their faces was remarkable. Both had crisp, black, tightly curling hair. Both had dark eyes and heavy eyebrows. Both had quick vivid complexions, slightly heightened by the sea and wind. But more striking than their similarity of colouring was the likeness of expression and bearing. Both wore the same air of picturesque energy, both bore themselves with a like graceful effrontery and self-possession.

The young man continued his way. The young girl lingered for a moment looking seaward, with her small brown hand lifted to shade her eyes,—a precaution which her heavy eyebrows and long lashes seemed to render utterly gratuitous.

'Come along, Mag. What are ye waitin' for?' said the young man impatiently.

'Nothin'. Lookin' at that boat from the Fort.' Her clear eyes were watching a small skiff, invisible to less keen-sighted observers, aground upon a flat near the mouth of the channel. 'Them chaps will have a high ole time gunnin' thar, stuck in the mud, and the tide goin' out like sixty!'

'Never you mind the sodgers,' returned her companion aggressively, 'they kin take care o' their own precious skins, or Uncle Sam will do it for 'em—I reckon. Anyhow the people—that's you and me, Mag—is expected to pay for their foolishness. That's what they're sent yer for. Ye oughter to be satisfied with that,' he added with deep sarcasm.

'I reckon they ain't expected to do much off o' dry land, and they can't help bein' queer on the water,' returned the young girl with a reflecting sense of justice.

'Then they ain't no call to go gunnin'—and wastin' Guv'ment powder on ducks instead o' Injuns.'

Thet's so,' said the girl, thoughtfully. 'Wonder ef Guv'ment pays for them frocks the Kernel's girls went cavortin' round Logport in last Sunday —they looked like a cirkis.'

'Like ez not the old Kernel gets it outer contracts—one way or another. *We* pay for it all the same,' he added gloomily.

'Jest the same ez if they were *my* clothes,' said the girl with a quick, fiery, little laugh, 'ain't it? Wonder how they'd like my sayin' that to 'em when they was prancin' round, eh, Jim?'

But her companion was evidently unprepared for this sweeping feminine deduction, and stopped it with masculine promptitude.

'Look yer—instead o' botherin' your head about what the Fort girls wear, you'd better trot along a little more lively. It's late enough now.'

'But these darned boots hurt like pizen,' said the girl, limping. 'They swallowed a lot o water over the tops while I was wadin' down there, and my feet go swashin' around like in a churn every step.'

'Lean on me, baby,' he returned, passing his arm around her waist, and dropping her head smartly on his shoulder. 'Thar.' The act was brotherly and slightly contemptuous, but it was sufficient to at once establish their kinship.

They continued on thus for some moments in silence, the girl, I fear, after the fashion of her sex, taking the fullest advantage of this slightly sentimental and caressing attitude. They were moving now along the edge of the Marsh, parallel with the line of rapidly fading horizon, following some trail only known to their keen youthful eyes. It was growing darker and darker. The cries of the sea-birds had ceased; even the call of a belated plover had died away inland; the hush of death lay over the black funereal pall of marsh at their side. The tide had run out with the day. Even the sea-breeze had lulled in this dead slack water of all Nature, as if waiting outside the bar with the ocean, the stars, and the night.

Suddenly the girl stopped, and halted her companion. The faint far sound of a bugle broke the silence, if the idea of interruption could have been conveyed by the two or three exquisite vibrations that seemed born of that silence itself, and to fade and die in it without break or discord. Yet it was only the 'retreat' call from the Fort, two miles distant and invisible.

The young girl's face had become irradiated, and her small mouth half opened as she listened. 'Do you know, Jim,' she said with a confidential sigh, 'I allus put words to that when I hear it— it's so pow'ful pretty. It allus goes to me like this: "Goes the day, Far away, With the light,

And the night Comes along—Comes along—Comes along—Like a-a-so-o-ong."' She here lifted her voice, a sweet, fresh, boyish contralto, in such an admirable imitation of the bugle that her brother, after the fashion of more select auditors, was, for a moment, quite convinced that the words meant something. Nevertheless, as a brother, it was his duty to crush this weakness. 'Yes, and it says: "Shut your head, Go to bed,"' he returned irascibly, 'and *you'ld* better come along, if we're goin' to hev any supper. There's Yeller Bob hez got ahead of us over there with the game already.'

The girl glanced towards a slouching, burdened figure that now appeared to be preceding them, straightened herself suddenly, and then looked attentively towards the Marsh.

'Not the sodgers again?' said her brother impatiently.

'No,' said the girl quickly, 'but if that don't beat anythin'! I'd hev sworn, Jim, that Yeller Bob was somewhere behind us. I saw him only jest now when "Taps" sounded, somewhere over thar.' She pointed with a half-uneasy expression in quite another direction from that in which the slouching Yellow Bob had just loomed.

'Tell ye what, Mag, makin' poetry outer bugle calls hez kinder muddled ye. *That's* Yeller Bob ahead, and ye orter know Injins well enuff by this time to remember that they allus crop up jest when ye don't expect them. And there's the bresh jest afore us. Come!'

The 'bresh,' or low bushes, was really a line of stunted willows and alders that seemed to have gradually sunk into the level of the plain, but increased in size farther inland, until they grew to the height and density of a wood. Seen from the channel it had the appearance of a green cape or promontory thrust upon the Marsh. Passing through its tangled recesses, with the aid of some unerring instinct, the two companions emerged upon another and much larger level that seemed as illimitable as the bay. The strong breath of the ocean lying just beyond the bar and estuary they were now facing came to them salt and humid as another tide. The nearer expanse of open water reflected the after-glow, and lightened the landscape. And between the two wayfarers and the horizon rose, bleak and startling, the strange outlines of their home.

At first it seemed a ruined colonnade of

many pillars, whose base and pediment were buried in the earth, supporting a long parallelogram of entablature and cornices. But a second glance showed it to be a one-storied building, upheld above the Marsh by numberless piles placed at regular distances; some of them sunken or inclined from the perpendicular, increasing the first illusion. Between these pillars, which permitted a free circulation of air and, at extraordinary tides, even the waters of the bay itself, the level waste of marsh, the bay, the surges of the bar, and finally the red horizon line were distinctly visible. A railed gallery or platform, supported also on piles, and reached by steps from the Marsh, ran around the building, and gave access to the several rooms and offices.

But if the appearance of this lacustrine and amphibious dwelling was striking, and not without a certain rude and massive grandeur, its grounds and possessions through which the brother and sister were still picking their way were even more grotesque and remarkable. Over a space of half a dozen acres the flotsam and jetsam of years of tidal offerings were collected, and even guarded with a certain care. The blackened hulks of huge uprooted trees scarcely distinguishable from the fragments of genuine wrecks beside them were securely fastened by chains to stakes and piles driven in the marsh while heaps of broken and disjointed bamboo orange crates, held together by ropes of fibre, glistened like ligamented bones heaped in the dead valley. Masts, spars, fragments of shell-encrusted boats, binnacles, round houses, and galleys, and part of the after-deck of a coasting schooner, had ceased their wanderings and found rest in this vast cemetery of the sea. The legend on a wheel-house, the lettering on a stern or bow served for mortuary inscription. Wailed over by the trade winds, mourned by lamenting sea-birds, once every year the tide visited its lost dead and left them wet with its tears.

To such a spot and its surroundings the atmosphere of tradition and mystery was not wanting. Six years ago Boone Culpepper had built the house, and brought to it his wife— variously believed to be a gypsy, a Mexican, a bright mulatto, a Digger Indian, a South Sea princess from Tahiti, somebody else's wife—but in reality a little Creole woman from New Orleans, with whom he had contracted a marriage, with other gambling debts, during a winter's vacation from his home in Virginia. At the end of two years she had died, succumbing, as differently stated, from perpetual wet feet, or the misanthropic idiosyncrasies of her husband, and leaving behind her a girl of twelve and a boy of sixteen to console him. How futile was this bequest may be guessed from a brief summary of Mr. Culpepper's peculiarities. They were the development of a singular form of aggrandisement and misanthropy. On his arrival at Logport he had bought a part of the apparently valueless Dedlow Marsh from the Government at less than a dollar an acre, continuing his singular investment year by year until he was the owner of three leagues of amphibious domain. It was then discovered that this property carried with it the *water front* of divers valuable and convenient sites for manufactures and the commercial ports of a noble bay, as well as the natural *embarcaderos* of some 'lumbering' inland settlements. Boone Culpepper would not sell. Boone Culpepper would not rent or lease. Boone Culpepper held an invincible blockade of his neighbours, and the progress and improvement he despised—granting only, after a royal fashion, occasional licence, revocable at pleasure, in the shape of tolls, which amply supported him, with the game he shot in his kingfisher's eyrie on the Marsh. Even the Government that had made him powerful was obliged to 'condemn' a part of his property at an equitable price for the purposes of Fort Redwood, in which the adjacent town of Logport shared. And Boone Culpepper, unable to resist the act, refused to receive the compensation or quit claim the town. In his scant intercourse with his neighbours he always alluded to it as his own, showed it to his children as part of their strange inheritance, and exhibited the starry flag that floated from the Fort as a flaunting insult to their youthful eyes. Hated, feared, and superstitiously shunned by some, regarded as a madman by others, familiarly known as 'The Kingfisher of Dedlow,' Boone Culpepper was one day found floating dead in his skiff, with a charge of shot through his head and shoulders. The shot gun lying at his feet at the bottom of the boat indicated the 'accident' as recorded in the verdict of the coroner's jury—but not by the people. A thousand rumours of murder or suicide prevailed, but always with the universal rider, 'Served him right.' So invincible was this feeling that but few attended his last rites, which took place at high water. The delay of the officiating clergyman lost the tide; the homely catafalque—his own boat—was left aground on the Marsh, and deserted by all mourners except the two children. Whatever he had instilled into them by precept and example, whatever took place that night in their lonely watch by his bier on the black marshes, it was certain that those who confidently looked for any change in the administration of the Dedlow Marsh were cruelly mistaken. The old Kingfisher was dead, but he had left in the nest two young birds, more beautiful and graceful, it was true, yet as fierce and tenacious of beak and talon.

II

Arriving at the house the young people ascended the outer flight of wooden steps which bore an odd likeness to the companion-way of a vessel, and the gallery, or 'deck,' as it was called—where a number of nets, floats, and buoys thrown over the railing completed the nautical resemblance. This part of the building was evidently devoted to kitchen, dining-room, and domestic offices; the principal room in the centre, serving as hall or living room, and communicating on the other side with two sleeping apartments. It was of considerable

size, with heavy lateral beams across the ceiling
— built, like the rest of the house, with a
certain maritime strength — and looked not
unlike a saloon cabin. An enormous open
Franklin stove between the windows, as large
as a chimney, blazing with drift wood, gave light
and heat to the apartment, and brought into
flickering relief the boarded walls hung with
the spoils of sea and shore, and glittering with
gun-barrels. Fowling-pieces of all sizes, from
the long ducking-gun mounted on a swivel for
boat use to the light single-barrel or carbine,
stood in racks against the walls; game-bags,
revolvers in their holsters, hunting and fishing
knives in their sheaths, depended from hooks
above them. In one corner stood a harpoon;
in another two or three Indian spears for

salmon. The carpetless floor and rude chairs and settles were covered with otter, mink, beaver, and a quantity of valuable sealskins, with a few larger pelts of the bear and elk. The only attempt at decoration was the displayed wings and breasts of the wood and harlequin duck, the muir, the cormorant, the gull, the gannet, and the femininely delicate half mourning of petrel and plover, nailed against the wall. The influence of the sea was dominant above all, and asserted its saline odours even through the spice of the drift wood smoke that half veiled the ceiling.

A berry-eyed old Indian woman with the complexion of dried salmon; her daughter also with berry eyes, and with a face that seemed wholly made of a moist laugh; 'Yellow Bob,' a Digger 'buck,' so called from the prevailing ochre markings of his cheek, and 'Washooh,' an ex-chief, a nondescript in a blanket, looking like a cheap and dirty doll whose fibrous hair was badly nailed on his carved wooden head, composed the Culpepper household. While the two former were preparing supper in the adjacent dining-room, Yellow Bob, relieved of his burden of game, appeared on the gallery and beckoned mysteriously to his master through the window. James Culpepper went out, returned quickly, and after a minute's hesitation and an uneasy glance towards his sister, who had meantime pushed back her sou'wester from her forehead, and without taking off her jacket had dropped into a chair before the fire with her back towards him, took his gun noiselessly from the rack, and saying carelessly that he would be back in a moment, disappeared.

Left to herself, Maggie coolly pulled off her long boots and stockings, and comfortably opposed to the fire two very pretty feet and ankles, whose delicate purity were slightly blue-bleached by confinement in the tepid sea water. The contrast of their waxen whiteness with her blue woollen skirt, and with even the skin of her sunburnt hands and wrists, apparently amused her, and she sat for some moments with her elbows on her knees, her skirts slightly raised, contemplating them, and curling her toes with evident satisfaction. The firelight playing upon the rich colouring of her face, the fringe of jet black curls that almost met the thick sweep of eyebrows, and left her only a white strip of forehead, her short upper lip and small chin, rounded but resolute, completed a piquant and striking figure. The rich brown shadows on the smoke-stained walls and ceiling, the occasional starting into relief of the scutcheons of brilliant plumage, and the momentary glitter of the steel barrels, made a quaint background to this charming picture. Sitting there, and following some lingering memory of her tramp on the Marsh, she hummed to herself a few notes of the bugle call that had impressed her— at first softly, and finally with the full pitch of her voice.

Suddenly she stopped.

There was a faint and unmistakable rapping on the floor beneath her. It was distinct, but cautiously given, as if intended to be audible to her alone. For a moment she stood upright, her feet still bare and glistening, on the otter skin that served as a rug. There were two doors to the room, one from which her brother had disappeared, which led to the steps, the other giving on the back gallery, looking inland. With a quick instinct she caught up her gun and ran to that one, but not before a rapid scramble near the railing was followed by a cautious opening of the door. She was just in time to shut it on the extended arm and light blue sleeve of an army overcoat that protruded through the opening, and for a moment threw her whole weight against it.

'A dhrop of whisky, Miss, for the love of God.'

She retained her hold, cocked her weapon,

and stepped back a pace from the door. The blue sleeve was followed by the rest of the overcoat, and a blue cap with the infantry blazoning, and the letter 'H' on its peak. They were for the moment more distinguishable than the man beneath them—grimed and blackened with the slime of the marsh. But what could be seen of his mud-stained face was more grotesque than terrifying. A combination of weakness and audacity, insinuation and timidity struggled through the dirt for expression. His small blue eyes were not ill-natured, and even the intruding arm trembled more from exhaustion than passion.

'On'y a dhrop, Miss,' he repeated piteously, 'and av ye pleeze, quick! afore I'm starved with the cold entoirely.'

She looked at him intently—without lowering her gun.

'Who are you?'

'Then, it's the truth I'll tell ye, Miss—whisht then!' he said in a half whisper; 'I'm a desarter!'

'Then it was *you* that was doggin' us on the Marsh?'

'It was the sarjint I was lavin', Miss.'

She looked at him hesitatingly.

'Stay outside there—if you move a step into the room, I'll blow you out of it.'

He stepped back on the gallery. She closed the door, bolted it, and still holding the gun, opened a cupboard, poured out a glass of whisky, and returning to the door, opened it and handed him the liquor.

She watched him drain it eagerly, saw the fiery stimulant put life into his shivering frame, trembling hands, and kindle his dull eye—and —quietly raised her gun again.

'Ah, put it down, Miss, put it down! Fwhot's the use? Sure the bullets yee carry in them oiyes of yours is more deadly! It's out here oi'll sthand, glory be to God, all night, without movin' a fut till the sarjint comes to take me, av ye won't levil them oiyes at me like that. Ah, whirra! look at that now! but it's a gooddess she is—the livin' Jaynus of warr, standin' there like a statoo, wid her alybaster fut put forward.'

In her pride and conscious superiority, any suggestion of shame at thus appearing before a common man and a mendicant, was as impossible to her nature as it would have been to a queen or the goddess of his simile. His presence and his compliment alike passed her calm modesty unchallenged. The wretched scamp recognised the fact and felt its power, and it was with a superstitious reverence asserting itself through his native extravagance that he raised his grimy hand to his cap in military salute and became respectfully rigid.

'Then the sodgers were huntin' *you?*' she said thoughtfully, lowering her weapon.

'Thrue for you, Miss—they worr, and it's meself that was lyin' flat in the ditch wid me faytures makin' an illigant cast in the mud—more betoken, as ye see even now—and the sarjint and his daytail thrampin' round me. It was thin that the mortial could sthruck thro' me mouth, and made we wake for the whisky that would resthore me.'

'What did you desert fer?'

'Ah, list to that now! Fwhot did I desart fer? Shure ev there was the ghost of an inemy round, it's meself that would be in the front now! But it was the letthers from me ould mother, Miss, that is sthruck wid a mortial illness—long life to her—in County Clare, and me sisthers in Ninth Avenue in New York, fornint the daypo, that is brekken their harruts over me listin' in the Fourth Infanthry to do duty in a haythen wilderness. Av it was the cavalry—and it's me own father that was in the Innishkillen Dthragoons, Miss—oi wouldn't moind. Wid a horse betune me legs, it's on parade oi'd be now, Miss, and not wandhering over the bare flure of the Marsh, stharved wid the cold, the thirst, and hunger, wid the mud and the moire thick on me; facin' an illigant young leddy as is the ekal ov a Fayld Marshal's darter—not to sphake ov Kernal Preston's—ez couldn't hold a candle to her.'

Brought up on the Spanish frontier, Maggie Culpepper was one of the few American girls who was not familiar with the Irish race. The rare smile that momentarily lit up her petulant mouth seemed to justify the intruder's praise. But it passed quickly, and she returned drily—

'That means you want more drink, suthin' to eat, and clothes. Suppose my brother comes back and ketches you here?'

'Shure, Miss, he's just now hunten me, along wid his two haythen Diggers, beyond the laygoon there. It worr the yellar one that sphotted me lyin' there in the ditch; it worr only your own oiyes, Miss—more power to their beauty for that—that saw me folly him unbeknownst here; and that desaved them, ye see!'

The young girl remained for an instant silent and thoughtful.

'We're no friends of the Fort,' she said finally, ' but I don't reckon for that reason my brother will cotton to *you*. Stay out thar where ye are, till I come to ye. If you hear me singin' again, you'll know he's come back, and ye'd better scoot with what you've already got, and be thankful.'

She shut the door again and locked it, went into the dining-room, returned with some provisions wrapped in paper, took a common wicker flask from the wall, passed into her brother's bedroom, and came out with a flannel shirt, 'overalls,' and a coarse Indian blanket, and, reopening the door, placed them before the astonished and delighted vagabond. His eye glistened; he began, 'Glory be to God,' but for once his habitual extravagance failed him. Nature triumphed with a more eloquent silence over his well-worn art. He hurriedly wiped his begrimed face and eyes with the shirt she had given him, and catching the sleeve of her rough pea-jacket in his dirty hand, raised it to his lips.

'Go!' she said imperiously. 'Get away while you can.'

'Av it was me last words—it's speechless oi am,' he stammered, and disappeared over the railing.

She remained for a moment holding the door half open, and gazing into the darkness that seemed to flow in like a tide. Then she shut it, and going into her bedroom resumed her interrupted toilette. When she emerged again she was smartly stockinged and slippered, and even the blue serge skirt was exchanged for a bright print, with a white *fichu* tied around her throat. An attempt to subdue her rebellious curls had resulted in the construction from their ruins of a low Norman arch across her forehead with pillared abutments of ringlets. When her brother returned a few moments later she did not look up, but remained, perhaps a little ostentatiously, bending over the fire.

'Bob allowed that the Fort boat was huntin'

men—deserters, I reckon,' said Jim aggrievedly. 'Wanted me to believe that he *saw* one on the Marsh hidin'. On'y an Injin lie, I reckon, to git a little extra fire-water, for toting me out to the bresh on a fool's errand.'

'Oh, *that's* where you went,' said Maggie, addressing the fire. 'Since when hev you tuk partnership with the Guv'nment and Kernel Preston to hunt up and take keer of their property?'

'Well, I ain't goin' to hev such wreckage as they pick up and enlist set adrift on our marshes, Mag,' said Jim decidedly.

'What would you hev done had you ketched him?' said Maggie, looking suddenly into her brother's face.

'Given him a dose of snipe shot that he'd

remember, and be thankful it wasn't slugs,' said Jim promptly. Observing a deeper seriousness in her attitude, he added, 'Why, if it was in war-time he'd get a *ball* from them sodgers on sight.'

'Yes, but *you* ain't got no call to interfere,' said Maggie.

'Ain't I? Why, he's no better than an outlaw. I ain't sure that he hasn't been stealin' or killin' somebody over theer.'

'Not *that* man!' said Maggie impulsively.

'Not what man?' said her brother, facing her quickly.

'Why,' returned Maggie, repairing her indiscretion with feminine dexterity, 'not *any* man who might have knocked you and me over on the marshes in the dusk, and grabbed our guns.'

'Wish he'd hev tried it,' said the brother, with a superior smile, but a quickly rising colour. 'Where d'ye suppose *I'd* hev been all the while?'

Maggie saw her mistake, and for the first time in her life resolved to keep a secret from her brother—overnight. 'Supper's gettin' cold,' she said, rising.

They went into the dining-room—an apartment as plainly furnished as the one they had quitted—but in its shelves, cupboards, and closely fitting boarding bearing out the general nautical suggestion of the house—and seated themselves before a small table on which their frugal meal was spread. In this *tête-à-tête* position Jim suddenly laid down his knife and fork and stared at his sister.

'Hello!'

'What's the matter?' said Maggie, starting slightly. 'How you do skeer one.'

'Who's been prinkin', eh?'

'My ha'r was in kinks all along o' that hat,' said Maggie, with a return of higher colour, 'and I had to straighten it. It's a boy's hat, not a girl's.'

'But that necktie and that gown—and all those frills and tuckers?' continued Jim generalising, with a rapid twirling of his fingers over her. 'Are you expectin' Judge Martin, or the Expressman, this evening?'

Judge Martin was the lawyer of Logport, who had proven her father's will, and had since raved about his single interview with the Kingfisher's beautiful daughter; the Expressman was a young fellow who was popularly supposed to have left his heart while delivering another valuable package on Maggie in person, and had 'never been the same man since.' It was a well-worn fraternal pleasantry that had done duty many a winter's evening, as a happy combination of moral admonition and cheerfulness. Maggie usually paid it the tribute of a quick little laugh and a sisterly pinch, but that evening those marks of approbation were withheld.

'Jim, dear,' said she, when their Spartan repast was concluded and they were re-established before the living-room fire. 'What was it the Redwood Mill Kempany offered you for that piece near Dead Man's Slough?'

Jim took his pipe from his lips long enough to say, 'Ten thousand dollars,' and put it back again.

'And what do ye kalkilate all our property, letting alone this yer house, and the driftwood front, is worth all together?'

'Includin' wot the Gov'nment owes us?—for that's all ours, ye know?' said Jim quickly.

'No—leavin' that out—jest for greens, you know,' suggested Maggie.

'Well, nigh onter a hundred and seventy-five thousand dollars, I reckon, by and large.'

'That's a heap o' money, Jim! I reckon old Kernel Preston wouldn't raise that in a hundred years,' continued Maggie, warming her knees by the fire.

'In five million years,' said Jim, promptly sweeping away further discussion. After a pause he added, 'You and me, Mag, kin see anybody's pile, and go 'em fifty thousand better.'

There were a few moments of complete silence, in which Maggie smoothed her knees, and Jim's pipe, which seemed to have become gorged and apoplectic with its owner's wealth, snored unctuously.

'Jim, dear, what if—it's on'y an idea of mine, you know—what if you sold that piece to the Redwood Mill, and we jest tuk that money and —and—and jest lifted the ha'r offer them folks at Logport? Jest as-tonished 'em! Jest tuk the best rooms in that new hotel, got a hoss and buggy, dressed ourselves, you and me, fit to kill, and made them Fort people take a back seat in the Lord's Tabernacle, oncet for all. You see what I mean, Jim,' she said hastily, as her brother seemed to be succumbing, like his pipe, in apoplectic astonishment, 'jest on'y to *show* 'em what we *could* do if we keerd. Lord! when we done it and spent the money we'd jest snap our fingers and skip back yer ez nat'ral ez life! Ye don't think, Jim,' she said, suddenly turning half fiercely upon him, 'that I'd allow to *live* among 'em—to stay a menet after that!'

Jim laid down his pipe and gazed at his sister with stony deliberation. 'And—what—do—you—kalkilate—to make by all that?' he said with scornful distinctness.

'Why, jest to show 'em we *have* got money, and could buy 'em all up if we wanted to,' returned Maggie, sticking boldly to her guns, albeit with a vague conviction that her fire was weakened through elevation, and somewhat alarmed at the deliberation of the enemy.

'And you mean to say they don't know it now,' he continued with slow derision.

'No,' said Maggie. 'Why, theer's that new school marm over at Logport, you know, Jim, the one that wanted to take your picter in your boat for a young smuggler or fancy pirate or Eyetalian fisherman, and allowed that your handsomed some, and offered to pay you for sittin'—do you reckon *she'd* believe you owned the land her schoolhouse was built on. No! Lots of 'em don't. Lots of 'em thinks we're poor and low down — and them ez doesn't, thinks——'

'What?' asked her brother sharply.

'That we're *mean*.'

The quick colour came to Jim's cheek. 'So,' he said, facing her quickly, 'for the sake of a lot of riff-raff and scum that's drifted here around us—jest for the sake of cuttin' a swell before them — you'll go out among the hounds ez allowed your mother was a Spanish nigger or a kanaka, ez called your father a pirate and landgrabber, ez much as allowed he was shot by some one or killed himself a purpose, ez said you was a heathen and a looney because you didn't go to school or church along with their trash, ez kept away from Maw's sickness ez if it was small-pox, and Dad's fun'ral ez if he was a hoss-thief, and left you and me to watch his coffin on the marshes all night till the tide kem back. And now you—*you* that jined hands with me that night over our father lyin' there cold and despised — ez if he was a dead dog thrown up by the tide—and swore that ez long ez that tide ebbed and flowed it couldn't bring you to them, or them to you agin! You now want—what? What? Why, to go and cast your lot among 'em, and live among 'em, and join in their God-forsaken holler foolishness, and—and—and——'

'Stop! It's a lie! I *didn't* say that. Don't you dare to say it,' said the girl, springing to her feet, and facing her brother in turn, with flashing eyes.

For a moment the two stared at each other —it might have been as in a mirror, so perfectly were their passions reflected in each line, shade, and colour of the other's face. It was as if they had each confronted their own passionate and wilful souls, and were frightened. It had often occurred before, always with the same invariable ending. The young man's eyes lowered first; the girl's filled with tears.

'Well, ef ye didn't mean that, what did ye mean?' said Jim, sinking, with sullen apology, back into his chair.

'I—only—meant it — for — for — revenge!' sobbed Maggie.

'Oh!' said Jim, as if allowing his higher nature to be touched by this noble instinct. 'But I didn't jest see where the revenge kem in.'

'No? But never mind now, Jim,' said Maggie, ostentatiously ignoring, after the fashion of her sex, the trouble she had produced; 'but to think — that — that — you thought——' (sobbing).

'But I didn't, Mag——' (caressingly).

With this very vague and impotent conclusion, Maggie permitted herself to be drawn beside her brother, and for a few moments they plumed each other's ruffled feathers, and smoothed each other's lifted crests like two beautiful young specimens of that halcyon genus to which they were popularly supposed to belong. At the end of half an hour Jim rose, and, yawning slightly, said in a perfunctory way—

'Where's the book?'

The book in question was the Bible. It had been the self-imposed custom of these two young people to read aloud a chapter every night as their one vague formula of literary and religious discipline. When it was produced Maggie, presuming on his affectionate and penitential condition, suggested that to-night he should pick out 'suthin' interestin'.' But this unorthodox frivolity was sternly put aside by Jim—albeit, by way of compromise, he agreed to 'chance it' —*i.e.*, open its pages at random.

He did so. Generally he allowed himself a moment's judicious pause for a certain chaste preliminary inspection necessary before reading aloud to a girl. To-night he omitted that modest precaution, and in a pleasant voice, which in reading was singularly free from colloquial infelicities of pronunciation, began at once—

'" Curse ye Meroz, said the angel of the Lord, curse ye bitterly the inhabitants thereof; because they came not to the help of the Lord, to the help of the Lord against the mighty."'

'Oh, you looked first,' said Maggie.

'I didn't now—honest Injin! I just opened.'

'Go on,' said Maggie, eagerly shoving him and interposing her neck over his shoulder.

And Jim continued Deborah's wonderful song of Jael and Sisera to the bitter end of its strong monosyllabic climax.

'There,' he said, closing the volume, 'that's what *I* call revenge. That's the real Scripture thing—no fancy frills theer.'

'Yes, but Jim, dear, don't you see that she treated him first—sorter got round him with free milk and butter, and reg'larly blandished him,' argued Maggie earnestly.

But Jim declined to accept this feminine suggestion, or to pursue the subject further, and after a fraternal embrace they separated for the night. Jim lingered long enough to look after the fastening of the door and windows, and Maggie remained for some moments at her casement, looking across the gallery to the Marsh beyond.

The moon had risen, the tide was half up. Whatever sign or trace of alien footprint or occupation had been there was already smoothly obliterated; even the configuration of the land had changed. A black cape had disappeared, a level line of shore had been eaten into by teeth of glistening silver. The whole dark surface of the Marsh was beginning to be streaked with shining veins as if a new life was coursing through it. Part of the open bay before the Fort, encroaching upon the shore, seemed in the moonlight to be reaching a white and outstretched arm towards the nest of the Kingfisher.

III

THE reveille at Fort Redwood had been supplemented full five minutes by the voice of Lieutenant George Calvert's servant, before that young officer struggled from his bed. His head was splitting, his tongue and lips were dry and feverish, his bloodshot eyes were shrinking from the insufferable light of the day, his mind a confused medley of the past night and the present morning, of cards and wild revelry, and the vision of a reproachfully trim orderly standing at his door with reports and orders which he now held composedly in his hand. For

Lieutenant Calvert had been enjoying a symposium, variously known as 'Stag Feed' and 'A Wild and Stormy Night,' with several of his brother officers, and a sickening conviction that it was not the first or the last time he had indulged in these festivities. At that moment he loathed himself, and then after the usual derelict fashion cursed the fate that had sent him, after graduating, to a frontier garrison—the dull monotony of whose duties made the Border horse-play of dissipation a relief. Already he had reached the miserable point of envying the veteran capacities of his superiors and equals. 'If I could drink like Kirby or Crowninshield, or if there was any other cursed thing a man could do in this hole,' he had wretchedly repeated to himself, after each misspent occasion, and yet already he was looking forward to them as part of a 'sub's' duty and worthy his emulation. Already the dream of social recreation fostered by West Point had been rudely dispelled. Beyond the garrison circle of Colonel Preston's family and two officers' wives, there was no society. The vague distrust and civil jealousy with which some frontier communities regard the Federal power, heightened in this instance by the uncompromising attitude the Government had taken towards the settlers' severe Indian policy had kept the people of Logport aloof from the Fort. The regimental band might pipe to them on Saturdays, but they would not dance.

Howbeit, Lieutenant Calvert dressed himself with uncertain hands but mechanical regularity and neatness, and, under the automatic training of discipline and duty, managed to button his tunic tightly over his feelings, to pull himself together with his sword-belt, compressing a still cadet-like waist, and to present that indescribable combination of precision and jauntiness which his brother officers too often allowed to lapse into frontier carelessness. His closely clipped light hair, yet dripping from a plunge in the cold water, had been brushed and parted with military exactitude, and when surmounted by his cap, with the peak in an artful suggestion of extra smartness tipped forward over his eyes, only his pale face—a shade lighter than his little blonde moustache—showed his last night's excesses. He was mechanically reaching for his sword and staring confusedly at the papers on his table when his servant interrupted—

'Major Bromley arranged that Lieutenant Kirby takes your sash this morning, as you're not well, sir, and you're to report for special to the colonel,' he added, pointing discreetly to the envelope.

Touched by this consideration of his superior, Major Bromley, who had been one of the veterans of last night's engagement, Calvert mastered the contents of the envelope without the customary anathema of specials, said—'Thank you, Parks,' and passed out on the verandah.

The glare of the quiet sunlit quadrangle, clean as a well-swept floor, the white-washed walls and galleries of the barrack buildings beyond, the white and green palisade of officers' cottages on either side, and the glitter of a sentry's bayonet, were for a moment intolerable to him. Yet, by a kind of subtle irony, never before had the genius and spirit of the vocation he had chosen seemed to be as incarnate as in the scene before him. Seclusion, self-restraint, cleanliness, regularity, sobriety, the atmosphere of a wholesome life, the austere reserve of a monastery without its mysterious or pensive meditation, were all there. To escape which he had of his own free will successively accepted a fool's distraction, the inevitable result of which was, the viewing of them the next morning with tremulous nerves and aching eyeballs.

An hour later, Lieutenant George Calvert had received his final instructions from Colonel Preston to take charge of a small detachment to recover and bring back certain deserters, but notably one, Dennis M'Caffrey of Company H, charged additionally with mutinous solicitation and example. As Calvert stood before his superior that distinguished officer, whose oratorical powers had been considerably stimulated through a long course of 'returning thanks for the Army,' slightly expanded his chest and said paternally—

'I am aware, Mr. Calvert, that duties of this kind are somewhat distasteful to young officers, and are apt to be considered in the light of police detail, but I must remind you that no one part of a soldier's duty can be held more important or honourable than another, and that the fulfilment of any one, however trifling, must, with honour to himself and security to his comrades, receive his fullest devotion. A sergeant and a file of men might perform your duty, but I require, in addition, the discretion, courtesy, and consideration of a gentleman who will command an equal respect from those with whom his duty brings him in contact. The unhappy prejudices which the settlers show to the military authority here, render this, as you are aware a difficult service, but I believe that you will, without forgetting the respect due to yourself and the Government you represent, avoid arousing these prejudices by any harshness, or inviting any conflict with the civil authority. The limits of their authority you will find in your written instructions, but you might gain their confidence and impress them, Mr. Calvert, with the idea of your being their *auxiliary* in the interests of justice—you understand. Even if you are unsuccessful in bringing back the men, you will do your best to ascertain if their escape has been due to the sympathy of the settlers, or even with their preliminary connivance. They may not be aware that inciting enlisted men to desert is a criminal offence; you will use your own discretion in informing them of the fact or not, as occasion may serve you. I have only to add, that while you are on the waters of this bay and the land covered by its tides, you have no opposition of authority, and are responsible to no one but your military superiors. Good-bye, Mr. Calvert. Let me hear a good account of you.'

Considerably moved by Colonel Preston's manner, which was as paternal and real as his rhetoric was somewhat perfunctory, Calvert half forgot his woes as he stepped from the commandant's piazza. But he had to face a group of his brother officers, who were awaiting him,—

'Good-bye, Calvert,' said Major Bromley, 'a day or two out on grass won't hurt you—and a change from Commissary whisky will put you all right. By the way, if you hear of any better stuff at Westport than they're giving us here, sample it and let us know. Take care of yourself. Give your men a chance to talk to you now and then, and you may get something from them, especially Donovan. Keep your eye on Ramon. You can trust your sergeant straight along.'

'Good-bye, George,' said Kirby. 'I suppose the old man told you that, although no part of a soldier's duty was better than another, your service was a very delicate one, just fitted for you, eh? He always does when he's cut out some hellish scrub-work for a chap. And told you, too, that as long as you didn't go ashore, and kept to a despatch-boat, or an eight-oared gig, where you couldn't deploy your men, or dress a line, you'd be invincible.'

'He did say something like that,' smiled Calvert, with an uneasy recollection, however, that it was *the* part of his superior's speech that particularly impressed him.

'Of course,' said Kirby gravely, '*that*, as an infantry officer, is clearly your duty.'

'And don't forget, George,' said Rollins still more gravely, 'that, whatever may befall you, you belong to a section of that numerically small but powerfully diversified organisation—

the American Army. Remember that in the hour of peril you can address your men in any language, and be perfectly understood. And remember that when you proudly stand before them, the eyes not only of your own country, but of nearly all the others, are upon you! Good-bye, Georgey. I heard the major hint something about whisky. They say that old pirate, Kingfisher Culpepper, had a stock of the real thing from Robertson County laid in his shebang on the Marsh just before he died. Pity we aren't on terms with them, for the cubs cannot drink it, and might be induced to sell. Shouldn't wonder, by the way, if your friend M'Caffrey was hanging round somewhere there; he always had a keen scent. You might confiscate it as an "incitement to desertion," you know. The girl's pretty, and ought to be growing up now.'

But haply at this point the sergeant stopped further raillery by reporting the detachment ready; and drawing his sword, Calvert, with a confused head, a remorseful heart, but an unfaltering step, marched off his men on his delicate mission.

It was four o'clock when he entered Jonesville. Following a matter-of-fact idea of his own, he had brought his men the greater distance by a circuitous route through the woods, thus avoiding the ostentatious exposure of his party on the open bay in a well-manned boat to an extended view from the three leagues of shore and marsh opposite. Crossing the stream, which here separated him from the

Dedlow Marsh by the common ferry, he had thus been enabled to halt unperceived below the settlement and occupy the two roads by which the fugitives could escape inland. He had deemed it not impossible that after the previous visit of the sergeant, the deserters hidden in the vicinity might return to Jonesville in the belief that the visit would not be repeated so soon. Leaving a part of his small force to patrol the road and another to deploy over the upland meadows, he entered the village. By the exercise of some boyish diplomacy and a certain prepossessing grace, which he knew when and how to employ, he became satisfied that the objects of his quest were not *there*—however, their whereabouts might have been known to the people. Dividing his party again, he concluded to take a corporal and a few men and explore the lower marshes himself.

The preoccupation of duty, exercise, and perhaps above all the keen stimulus of the iodine-laden salt air seemed to clear his mind and invigorate his body. He had never been in the Marsh before, and enjoyed its novelty with the zest of youth. It was the hour when the tide of its feathered life was at its flood. Clouds of duck and teal passing from the fresh water of the river to the salt pools of the marshes perpetually swept his path with flying shadows; at times it seemed as if even the uncertain ground around him itself arose and sped away on dusky wings. The vicinity of hidden pools and sloughs were betrayed by startled splashings; a few paces from their marching feet arose the sunlit pinions of a swan. The air was filled with multitudinous small cries and pipings. In this vocal confusion it was some minutes before he recognised the voice of one of his out-flankers calling to the other.

An important discovery had been made. In a long tongue of bushes that ran down to the Marsh they had found a mud-stained uniform, complete even to the cap, bearing the initial of the deserter's company.

'Is there any hut or cabin hereabouts Schmidt?' asked Calvert.

'Dot vos schoost it, Lefdennun,' replied his corporal. 'Dot vos de shanty from der King-visher—old Gulbebber. I pet a dollar, py shimminy, dot der men haf der gekommt.'

He pointed through the brake to a long low

building that now raised itself, white in the sunlight, above the many blackened piles. Calvert saw, in a single reconnoitring glance, that it had but one approach—the flight of steps from the Marsh. Instructing his men to fall in on the outer edge of the brake and await his orders, he quickly made his way across the space and ascended the steps. Passing along the gallery he knocked at the front door. There was no response. He repeated his knock. Then the window beside it opened suddenly, and he was confronted with the double-muzzle of a long ducking gun. Glancing instinctively along the barrels, he saw at their other extremity the bright eyes, brilliant colour, and small set mouth of a remarkably handsome girl. It was the fact, and to the credit of his training, that he paid more attention to the eyes than to the challenge of the shining tubes before him.

'Jest stop where you are—will you!' said the girl determinedly.

Calvert's face betrayed not the slightest terror or surprise. Immovable as on parade, he carried his white gloved hand to his cap, and said gently, 'With pleasure.'

'Oh yes,' said the girl quickly, 'but if you move a step I'll jest blow you and your gloves offer that railin' inter the Marsh.'

'I trust not,' returned Calvert, smiling.

'And why?'

'Because it would deprive me of the pleasure of a few moments' conversation with you—and I've only one pair of gloves with me.'

He was still watching her beautiful eyes—

respectfully, admiringly, and strategically. For he was quite convinced that if he *did* move she would certainly discharge one or both barrels at him.

'Where's the rest of you?' she continued sharply.

'About three hundred yards away, in the covert, not near enough to trouble you.'

'Will they come here?'

'I trust not.'

'You trust not?' she repeated scornfully. 'Why?'

'Because they would be disobeying orders.'

She lowered her gun slightly, but kept her black brows levelled at him. 'I reckon I'm a match for *you*,' she said with a slightly contemptuous glance at his slight figure, and opened the door. For a moment they stood looking at each other. He saw, besides the handsome face and eyes that had charmed him, a tall slim figure, made broader across the shoulders by an open pea-jacket that showed a man's red flannel shirt belted at the waist over a blue skirt, with the collar knotted by a sailor's black handkerchief, and turned back over a pretty though sunburnt throat. She saw a rather undersized young fellow in a jaunty undress uniform, scant of gold braid, and bearing only the single gold shoulder-bars of his rank, but scrupulously neat and well fitting. Light-coloured hair cropped close, the smallest of light moustaches, clear and penetrating blue eyes, and a few freckles completed a picture that did not prepossess her. She was therefore the more inclined to resent the perfect ease and self-possession with which the stranger carried off these manifest defects before her.

She laid aside the gun, put her hands deep in the pockets of her pea-jacket, and, slightly squaring her shoulders, said curtly, 'What do you want?'

'A very little information, which I trust it will not trouble you to give me. My men have just discovered the uniform belonging to a deserter from the Fort lying in the bushes yonder. Can you give me the slightest idea how it came there?'

'What right have you trapseing over our property?' she said, turning upon him sharply with a slight paling of colour.

'None whatever.'

'Then what did you come for?'

'To ask that permission, in case you would give me no information.'

'Why don't you ask my brother, and not a woman? Were you afraid?'

'He could hardly have done me the honour of placing me in more peril than you have,' returned Calvert, smiling. 'Then I have the pleasure of addressing Miss Culpepper?'

'I'm Jim Culpepper's sister.'

'And, I believe, equally able to give or refuse the permission I ask.'

'And what if I refuse?'

'Then I have only to ask pardon for having troubled you, go back, and return here with the tide. You don't resist *that* with a shot-gun, do you?' he asked pleasantly.

Maggie Culpepper was already familiar with the accepted theory of the supreme jurisdiction of the Federal Sea. She half turned her back upon him, partly to show her contempt, but partly to evade the domination of his clear, good-humoured, and self-sustained little eyes.

'I don't know anythin' about your deserters, nor what rags o' theirs happen to be floated up here,' she said angrily, 'and don't care to. You kin do what you like.'

'Then I'm afraid I should remain here a little longer, Miss Culpepper, but my duty——'

'Your wot?' she interrupted disdainfully.

'I suppose I *am* talking shop,' he said smilingly. 'Then my business——'

'Your business—pickin' up half-starved runaways!'

'And, I trust, sometimes a kind friend,' he suggested with a grave bow.

'You *trust?* Look yer, young man,' she said with her quick, fierce, little laugh, 'I reckon you *trust* a heap too much!' She would like to have added, 'with your freckled face, red hair, and little eyes'—but this would have obliged her to face them again, which she did not care to do.

Calvert stepped back, lifted his hand to his cap, still pleasantly, and then walked gravely along the gallery, down the steps, and towards the cover. From her window, unseen, she followed his neat little figure moving undeviatingly on, without looking to the left or right, and still less towards the house he had just quitted. Then she saw the sunlight flash on cross-belt plates and steel barrels, and a light blue line issued from out the dark green bushes, round the point, and disappeared. And then it suddenly occurred to her what she had been doing! This, then, was her first step towards that fancy she had so lately conceived, quarrelled over with her brother, and lay awake last night to place anew, in spite of all opposition! This was her brilliant idea of dazzling and subduing Logport and the Fort! Had she grown silly, or what had happened? Could she have dreamed of the coming of this whipper-snapper, with his insufferable airs, after that beggarly deserter? I am afraid that for a few moments the miserable fugitive had as small a place in Maggie's sympathy as the redoubtable whipper-snapper himself. And now the cherished dream

of triumph and conquest was over! What a
'looney' she had been! Instead of inviting
him in, and outdoing him in 'company manners,'
and 'fooling' him about the deserter, and then
blazing upon him afterwards at Logport in the
glory of her first spent wealth and finery, she
had driven him away!

And now 'he'll go and tell—tell the Fort
girls of his hairbreadth escape from the claws
of the Kingfisher's daughter!'

The thought brought a few bitter tears to her
eyes, but she wiped them away. The thought
brought also the terrible conviction that
Jim was right, that there could be nothing
but open antagonism between them and the
traducers of their parents, as she herself
had instinctively shown! But she presently

wiped that conviction away also, as she had her tears.

Half an hour later she was attracted by the appearance from the windows of certain straggling blue spots on the upland that seemed moving diagonally towards the Marsh. She did not know that it was Calvert's second 'detail' joining him, but believed for a moment that he had not yet departed, and was strangely relieved. Still later the frequent disturbed cries of coot, heron, and marsh hen, recognising the presence of unusual invaders of their solitude, distracted her yet more, and forced her at last with increasing colour and an uneasy sense of shyness to steal out to the gallery for a swift furtive survey of the Marsh. But an utterly unexpected sight met her eyes, and kept her motionless.

The birds were rising everywhere and drifting away with querulous perturbation before a small but augmented blue detachment that was moving with monotonous regularity towards the point of bushes where she had seen the young officer previously disappear. In their midst, between two soldiers with fixed bayonets, marched the man whom even at that distance she instantly recognised as the deserter of the preceding night, in the very clothes she had given him. To complete her consternation, a little to the right marched the young officer also, but accompanied by, and apparently on the most amicable terms with, Jim—her own brother!

To forget all else and dart down the steps, flying towards the point of bushes, scarcely knowing why or what she was doing, was to

Maggie the impulse and work of a moment. When she had reached it the party were not twenty paces away. But here a sudden shyness and hesitation again seized her, and she shrank back in the bushes with an instinctive cry to her brother inarticulate upon her lips. They came nearer, they were opposite to her; her brother Jim keeping step with the invader, and even conversing with him with an animation she had seldom seen upon his face—they passed! She had been unnoticed, except by one. The roving eye of the deserter had detected her handsome face among the leaves, slightly turned towards it, and poured out his whole soul in a single swift wink of eloquent but indescribable confidence.

When they had quite gone, she crept back

to the house, a little reassured, but still tremulous. When her brother returned at nightfall, he found her brooding over the fire, in the same attitude as on the previous night.

'I reckon ye might hev seen me go by with the sodgers,' he said, seating himself beside her, a little awkwardly, and with an unusual assumption of carelessness.

Maggie, without looking up, was languidly surprised. He had been with the soldiers—and where?

'About two hours ago I met this yer Leftenant Calvert,' he went on, with increasing awkwardness, 'and—oh, I say, Mag—he said he saw you, and hoped he hadn't troubled ye, and—and—ye saw him, didn't ye?'

Maggie, with all the red of the fire concentrated in her cheek as she gazed at the flame, believed carelessly 'that she had seen a shrimp in uniform asking questions.'

'Oh, he ain't a bit stuck up,' said Jim quickly, 'that's what I like about him. He's as nat'ral ez you be, and tuck my arm, walkin' around, careless-like, laffen at what he was doin', ez ef it was a game, and he wasn't sole commander of forty men. He's only a year or two older than me—and—and——' he stopped and looked uneasily at Maggie.

'So ye've bin craw-fishin' agin?' said Maggie in her deepest and most scornful contralto.

'Who's craw-fishin'?' he retorted angrily.

'What's this backen' out o' what you said yesterday? What's all this trucklin' to the Fort now?'

'What? Well, now, look yer,' said Jim, rising suddenly, with reproachful indignation, 'darned if I don't jest tell ye everythin'. I promised *him* I wouldn't. He allowed it would frighten ye.'

'*Frighten me!*' repeated Maggie contemptuously, nevertheless with her cheek paling again. 'Frighten me—with what?'

'Well, since yer so cantankerous, look yer. We've been robbed!'

'Robbed?' echoed Maggie, facing him.

'Yes, robbed by that same deserter! Robbed of a suit of my clothes, and my whisky-flask, and the darned skunk had 'em on. And if it hadn't bin for that Leftenant Calvert, and my givin' him permission to hunt him over the Marsh, we wouldn't have caught him.'

'Robbed?' repeated Maggie again, vaguely.

'Yes, robbed! Last night, afore we came home. He must hev got in yer, while we was comin' from the boat.'

'Did—did, that Leftenant say so?' stammered Maggie.

'Say it, of course he did, and so do I,' continued Jim impatiently. 'Why, there were my very clothes on his back, and he daren't deny it. And if you'd hearkened to me jest now, instead of flyin' off in tantrums, you'd see that *that's* jest how we got him, and how me and the Leftenant joined hands in it. I didn't give him permission to hunt deserters, but *thieves*. I didn't help him to ketch the man that deserted from *him*, but the skunk that took *my* clothes. For when the Leftenant found the man's old uniform in the bush, he nat'rally kalkilated he must hev got some other duds near by in some underhand way. Don't you see? Eh? Why, look, Mag. Darned if you ain't skeered after all! Who'd hev thought it? There now—sit down, dear. Why, you're white ez a gull.'

He had his arm round her as she sank back in the chair again with a forced smile.

'There now,' he said with fraternal superiority, 'don't mind it, Mag, any more. Why, it's all over now. You bet he won't trouble us agin, for the Leftenant sez that now he's found out to be a thief, they'll jest turn him over to the police, and he's sure o' getten' six months' State prison fer stealin' and burglarin' in our house. But,' he stopped suddenly and looked at, his sister's contracted face. 'Look yer, Mag. You're sick, that's what's the matter. Take suthin'——'

'I'm better now,' she said with an effort, 'it's only a kind o' blind chill I must hev got on the Marsh last night. What's that?'

She had risen, and grasping her brother's arm tightly had turned quickly to the window. The casement had suddenly rattled.

'It's only the wind gettin' up. It looked like a sou'wester when I came in. Lot o' scud flyin'. But *you* take some quinine, Mag. Don't *you* go now and get down sick like Maw.'

Perhaps it was this well-meant but infelicitous reference that brought a moisture to her dark eyes, and caused her lips to momentarily quiver. But it gave way to a quick determined setting of her whole face as she turned it once more to the fire, and said slowly—

'I reckon I'll sleep it off, if I go to bed now. What time does the tide fall.'

'About three, unless this yer wind piles it up on the Marsh afore then. Why?'

'I was only wonderin' if the boat wus safe,' said Maggie, rising.

'You'd better hoist yourself outside some quinine, instead o' talken' about those things,' said Jim, who preferred to discharge his fraternal responsibility by active medication. 'You aren't fit to read to-night.'

'Good night, Jim,' she said suddenly, stopping before him.

'Good night, Mag.' He kissed her with protecting and amiable toleration, generously referring her hot hands and feverish lips to that vague mystery of feminine complaint which man admits without endorsing.

They separated. Jim, under the stimulus of the late supposed robbery, ostentatiously fastening the doors and windows with assuring comments, calculated to inspire confidence in his sister's startled heart. Then he went to bed. He lay awake long enough to be pleasantly conscious that the wind had increased to a gale, and to be lulled again to sleep by the cosy security of the heavily timbered and tightly sealed dwelling that seemed to ride the storm like the ship it resembled. The gale swept through the piles beneath him and along the gallery as through bared spars and over wave-washed decks. The whole structure, attacked above, below, and on all sides by the fury of the wind, seemed at times to be lifted in the air. Once or twice the creaking timbers simulated the sound of opening doors and passing footsteps, and again dilated as if the gale had forced a passage through. But Jim slept on peacefully, and was at last only aroused by the brilliant sunshine staring through his window from the clear wind-swept blue arch beyond.

Dressing himself lazily, he passed into the sitting-room, and proceeded to knock at his sister's door, as was his custom; he was amazed to find it open and the room empty. Entering hurriedly he saw that her bed was undisturbed, as if it had not been occupied and was the more bewildered to see a note ostentatiously pinned upon the pillow, addressed in pencil in a large school-girl hand, 'To Jim.'

Opening it impatiently, he was startled to read as follows:—

'Don't be angry, Jim dear—but it was all my fault —and I didn't tell you. I knew all about the deserter, and I gave him the clothes and things that they say he stole. It was while you was out that night, and he came and begged of me, and was mournful and hidjus to behold. I thought I was helping him, and getting our revenge on the Fort, all at the same time. Don't be mad, Jim dear, and don't be frighted fer me. I'm going over thar to make it all right—to free *him* of stealing—to have *you* left out of it all—and take it all on myself. Don't you be a bit feared for me. I ain't skeert of the wind or of going. I'll close reef everything, clear the creek, stretch across to Injen Island, hugg the Point, and bear up fer Logport. Dear Jim—don't get mad— but I couldn't bear this fooling of you nor *him*—and that man being took for stealing any longer !—Your loving sister, MAGGIE.'

With a confused mingling of shame, anger,

and sudden fear he ran out on the gallery. The tide was well up, half the Marsh had already vanished, and the little creek where he had moored his skiff was now an empty shining river. The water was everywhere—fringing the tussocks of salt grass with concentric curves of spume and drift, or tumultuously tossing its white-capped waves over the spreading expanse of the lower bay. The low thunder of breakers in the farther estuary broke monotonously on the ear. But his eye was fascinated by a dull shifting streak on the horizon that, even as he gazed, shuddered, whitened along its whole line, and then grew ghastly gray again. It was the ocean bar.

IV

'Well, I must say,' said Cicely Preston, emphasising the usual feminine imperative for perfectly gratuitous statement, as she pushed back her chair from the commandant's breakfast table, 'I *must* really say that I don't see anything particularly heroic in doing something wrong, lying about it just to get other folks into trouble, and then rushing off to do penance in a high wind and an open boat. But she's pretty, and wears a man's shirt and coat, and of course *that* settles anything. But why earrings and wet white stockings and slippers? And why that Gothic arch of front and a boy's hat? That's what I simply ask,' and the youngest daughter of Colonel Preston rose from the table, shook out the skirt of her pretty morning dress; and, placing her little thumbs in the belt of her smart waist, paused witheringly for a reply.

'You are most unfair, my child,' returned Colonel Preston gravely. 'Her giving food and clothes to a deserter may have been only an ordinary instinct of humanity towards a fellow-creature who appeared to be suffering, to say nothing of M'Caffrey's plausible tongue. But her perilling her life to save him from an unjust accusation, and her desire to shield her brother's pride from ridicule, is altogether praiseworthy and extraordinary. And the moral influence of her kindness was strong enough to make that scamp refuse to tell the plain truth that might implicate her in an indiscretion, though it saved him from State prison.'

'He knew you wouldn't believe him if he had said the clothes were given to him,' retorted Miss Cicely, 'so I don't see where the moral influence comes in. As to her perilling her life, those Marsh people are amphibious anyway, or would be in those clothes. And, as to her motive, why papa, I heard you say in this very room, and afterwards to Mr. Calvert, when you gave him instructions, that you believed those Culpeppers were capable of enticing away deserters; and you forget the fuss you had with her savage brother's lawyer about that water front, and how you said it was such people who kept up the irritation between the Civil and Federal power.'

The colonel coughed hurriedly. It is the fate of all great organisers, military as well as civil, to occasionally suffer defeat in the family circle.

'The more reason,' he said soothingly, 'why we should correct harsh judgments that spring from mere rumours. You should give yourself at least the chance of overcoming your prejudices, my child. Remember, too, that she is now the guest of the Fort.'

'And she chooses to stay with Mrs. Bromley! I'm sure it's quite enough for you and mamma to do duty—and Emily—who wants to know why Mr. Calvert raves so about her —without *my* going over there to stare.'

Colonel Preston shook his head reproachfully,

but eventually retired, leaving the field to the enemy. The enemy, a little pink in the cheeks, slightly tossed the delicate rings of its blonde crest, settled its skirts again at the piano, but after turning over the leaves of its music book, rose, and walked pettishly to the window.

But here a spectacle presented itself that for a moment dismissed all other thoughts from the girl's rebellious mind.

Not a dozen yards away on the wind-swept parade a handsome young fellow, apparently halted by the sentry, had impetuously turned upon him in an attitude of indignant and haughty surprise. To the quick fancy of the girl it seemed as if some disguised rustic god had been startled by the challenge of a mortal. Under an oilskin hat, like the *petasus* of

Hermes, pushed back from his white forehead crisp black curls were knotted around a head, whose beardless face was perfect as a cameo cutting. In the close-fitting blue-woollen jersey under his open jacket the clear outlines and youthful grace of his upper figure were revealed as clearly as in a statue. Long fishing-boots reaching to his thighs scarcely concealed the symmetry of his lower limbs. Cricket and lawn-tennis, knicker-bockers and flannels had not at that period familiarised the female eye to unfettered masculine outline, and Cicely Preston, accustomed to the artificial smartness and regularity of uniform, was perhaps the more impressed by the stranger's lawless grace.

The sentry had repeated his challenge; an angry flush was deepening on the intruder's cheek. At this critical moment Cicely threw open the French windows and stepped upon the verandah.

The sentry saluted the familiar little figure of his colonel's daughter with an explanatory glance at the stranger. The young fellow looked up—and the god became human.

I'm 'looking for my sister,' he said half awkwardly half defiantly—'she's here, somewhere.'

'Yes—and perfectly safe, Mr. Culpepper, I think'—said the arch-hypocrite with dazzling sweetness, 'and we're all so delighted. And so brave and plucky, and skilful in her to come all that way—and for such a purpose.'

'Then—you know—all about it'—stammered Jim, more relieved than he had imagined—'and that I——'

'That you were quite ignorant of your sister helping the deserter—Oh yes, of course,'—said Cicely with bewildering promptitude. 'You see, Mr. Culpepper, we girls are *so* foolish. I daresay *I* should have done the same thing in her place, only *I* should never have had the courage to do what she did afterwards. You really must forgive her. But won't you come in—*do*.' She stepped back, holding the window open with the half-coaxing air of a spoiled child. 'This way is quickest. *Do* come.' As he still hesitated, glancing from her to the house, she added, with a demure little laugh, 'Oh, I forget this is Colonel Preston's quarters, and I'm his daughter.'

And this dainty little fairy, so natural in manner, so tasteful in attire was one of the artificial overdressed creatures that his sister had —inveighed against so bitterly! Was Maggie really to be trusted? This new revelation coming so soon after the episode of the deserter staggered him. Nevertheless he hesitated—looking up with a certain boyish timidity into Cicely's dangerous eyes.

'Is—is—my sister there?'

'I'm expecting her with my mother every moment,' responded this youthful but ingenious diplomatist sweetly; 'she might be here now, but,' she added with a sudden heart-broken flash of sympathy, 'I know *how* anxious you both must be. *I'll* take you to her now. Only one moment, please.' The opportunity of leading this handsome savage as it were in chains across the parade, before everybody, her father,

her mother, her sister, and *his*—was not to be lost. She darted into the house, and reappeared with the daintiest imaginable straw hat on the side of her head, and demurely took her place at his side. 'It's only over there, at Major Bromley's,' she said, pointing to one of the vine-clad cottage quarters; 'but you are a stranger here, you know, and might get lost.'

Alas! he was already that. For keeping step with those fairy-like slippers, brushing awkwardly against that fresh and pretty skirt, and feeling the caress of the soft folds; looking down upon the brim of that beribboned little hat, and more often meeting the upturned blue eyes beneath it, Jim was suddenly struck with a terrible conviction of his own contrasting coarseness and deficiencies. How hideous those oiled canvas fishing trousers and pilot jacket looked beside this perfectly fitted and delicately gowned girl! He loathed his collar, his jersey, his turned-back sou'wester, even his height, which seemed to hulk beside her—everything, in short, that the girl had recently admired. By the time that they had reached Major Bromley's door he had so far succumbed to the fair enchantress and realised her ambition of a triumphant procession, that when she ushered him into the presence of half a dozen ladies and gentlemen he scarcely recognised his sister as the centre of attraction, or knew that Miss Cicely's effusive greeting of Maggie was her first one. 'I knew he was dying to see you after all you had *both* passed through, and I brought him straight here,' said the diminutive Machiavelli, meeting the astonished gaze of her father and the curious eyes of her sister with perfect calmness, while Maggie, full of gratitude and admiration of her handsome brother, forgot his momentary obliviousness, and returned her greeting warmly. Nevertheless, there was a slight movement of reserve among the gentlemen at the unlooked-for irruption of this sunburnt Adonis, until Calvert, disengaging himself from Maggie's side, came forward with his usual frank imperturbability and quiet tact, and claimed Jim as his friend and honoured guest.

It then came out with that unostentatious simplicity which characterised the brother and sister, and was their secure claim to perfect equality with their entertainers, that Jim, on discovering his sister's absence, and fearing that she might be carried by the current towards the bar, had actually *swam the estuary* to Indian Island, and in an ordinary Indian canoe had braved the same tempestuous passage she had taken a few hours before. Cicely, listening to this recital with rapt attention, nevertheless managed to convey the impression of having fully expected it from the first. 'Of course he'd have come here—if she'd only waited,' she said, *sotto voce*, to her sister Emily.

'He's certainly the handsomer of the two,' responded that young lady.

'Of course,' returned Cicely, with a superior air, 'don't you see she *copies* him.'

Not that this private criticism prevented either from vying with the younger officers in their attentions to Maggie, with perhaps the addition of an open eulogy of her handsome brother, more or less invidious in comparison to the officers. 'I suppose it's an active out-of-door life gives him that perfect grace and freedom,' said Emily with a slight sneer at the smartly belted Calvert. 'Yes, and he don't drink or keep late hours,' responded Cicely significantly. 'His sister says they always retire before ten o'clock, and that although his father left him some valuable whisky he seldom takes a drop of it.' 'Therein,' gravely concluded Captain Kirby, 'lies *our* salvation. If, after such a confession, Calvert doesn't make the most of his acquaintance with young Culpepper to remove that whisky from his path and bring it here, he's not the man I take him for.'

Indeed, for the moment it seemed as if he was not. During the next three or four days, in which Colonel Preston had insisted upon detaining his guests, Calvert touched no liquor, evaded the evening poker parties at quarters, and even prevailed upon some of his brother officers to give them up for the more general entertainment of the ladies. Colonel Preston was politician enough to avail himself of the popularity of Maggie's adventure to invite some of the Logport people to assist him in honouring their neighbour. Not only was the old feud between the Fort and the people thus bridged over, but there was no doubt that the discipline of the Fort had been strengthened by Maggie's extravagant reputation as a mediator among the disaffected rank and file. Whatever characteristic licence the grateful Dennis M'Caffrey—let off with a nominal punishment—may have taken in his praise of the 'Quane of the Marshes,' it is certain that the men worshipped her, and that the band pathetically begged permission to serenade her the last night of her stay.

At the end of that time, with a dozen invitations, a dozen appointments, a dozen vows of eternal friendship, much hand-shaking, and accompanied by a number of the officers to their boat, Maggie and Jim departed. They talked but little on their way home; by some tacit understanding they did not discuss those projects, only recalling certain scenes and incidents of their visit. By the time they had reached the little creek the silence and nervous apathy which usually follow excitement in the young seemed to have fallen upon them. It was not until after their quiet frugal supper that, seated beside the fire, Jim looked up somewhat self-consciously in his sister's grave and thoughtful face.

'Say, Mag, what was that idea o' your's about selling some land, and taking a house at Logport?'

Maggie looked up, and said passively, 'Oh, *that* idea?'

'Yes.'

'Why?'

'Well,' said Jim somewhat awkwardly, 'it *could* be done, you know. I'm willin'.'

As she did not immediately reply, he continued uneasily, 'Miss Preston says we kin get a nice little house that is near the Fort, until we want to build.'

'Oh, then you *have* talked about it?'

'Yes—that is—why, what are ye thinkin' of, Mag? Wasn't it *your* idea all along?' he said, suddenly facing her in querulous embarrassment. They had been sitting in their usual evening attitudes of Assyrian frieze profile, with even more than the usual Assyrian frieze similarity of feature.

'Yes—but, Jim, dear—do you think it the best thing for—for us to do?' said Maggie, with half-frightened gravity.

At this sudden and startling exhibition of female inconsistency and inconsequence, Jim was for a moment speechless. Then he recovered himself, volubly, aggrievedly, and on his legs.

What *did* she mean? Was he to give up understanding girls — or was it their sole vocation in life to impede masculine processes and shipwreck masculine conclusions? Here, after all she said the other night, after they had nearly 'quo'lled' over her 'set idees,' after she'd gone over all that foolishness about Jael and Sisera — and there wasn't any use for it — after she'd let him run on to them officers all he was goin' to do — nay, after *she* herself, for he had heard her, had talked to Calvert about it, she wanted to know *now*, if it was best! He looked at the floor and the ceiling, as if expecting the tongued and grooved planks to cry out at this crowning enormity.

The cause of it had resumed her sad gaze at the fire. Presently, without turning her head, she reached up her long graceful arm, and clasping her brother's neck, brought his face down in profile with her own, cheek against cheek, until they looked like the double outlines of a medallion. Then she said—to the fire,—

'Jim, do you think she's pretty?'

'Who?' said Jim, albeit his colour had already answered the question.

'You know *who*. Do you like her?'

Jim here vaguely murmured to the fire that he thought her 'kinder nice,' and that she dressed mighty purty. 'Ye know, Mag,' he said with patronising effusion, 'ye oughter get some gownds like her's.'

'That wouldn't make me like her,' said Maggie gravely.

'I don't know about that,' said Jim politely,

but with an appalling hopelessness of tone. After a pause he added slyly, "'Pears to me *somebody else* thought somebody else mighty purty—eh?'

To his discomfiture she did not solicit further information. After a pause he continued, still more archly—

'Do you like *him*, Mag?'

'I think he's a perfect gentleman,' she said calmly.

He turned his eyes quickly from the glowing fire to her face. The cheek that had been resting against his own was as cool as the night wind that came through the open door, and the whole face was as fixed and tranquil as the upper stars.

V

For a year the tide had ebbed and flowed on the Dedlow Marsh unheeded before the sealed and sightless windows of the 'Kingfisher's Nest.' Since the young birds had flown to Logport, even the Indian caretakers had abandoned the piled dwelling for their old nomadic haunts in the 'bresh.' The high spring-tide had again made its annual visit to the little cemetery of drift wood, and, as if recognising another wreck in the deserted home, had hung a few memorial offerings on the blackened piles, softly laid a garland of grayish drift before it, and then sobbed itself out in the salt grass.

From time to time faint echoes of the Culpeppers' life at Logport reached the upland, and the few neighbours who had only known them by hearsay shook their heads over the extravagance they as yet only knew by report. But it was in the dead ebb of the tide and the waning daylight that the feathered tenants of the Marsh seemed to voice dismal prophecies of the ruin of their old master and mistress, and to give themselves up to gloomiest lamentation and querulous foreboding. Whether the traditional 'bird of the air' had entrusted his secret to a few ornithological friends, or whether from a natural disposition to take gloomy views of life, it was certain that at this hour the vocal expression of the Marsh was hopeless and despairing. It was then that a dejected plover, addressing a mocking crew of sand-pipers on a floating log, seemed to bewail the fortune that was being swallowed up by the riotous living and gambling debts of Jim. It was then that the querulous crane rose, and testily protested against the selling of his favourite haunt in the sandy peninsula, which only six months of Jim's excesses had made imperative. It was then that a mournful curlew, who, with the preface that he had always been really expecting it, reiterated the story that Jim had been seen more than once staggering home with nervous hands and sodden features from a debauch with the younger officers; it was the same desponding fowl who knew that Maggie's eyes had more than once filled with tears at Jim's failings, and had already grown more hollow with many watchings. It was a flock of wrangling teal that screamingly discussed the small scandals, jealous heart-burnings, and curious backbitings that had attended Maggie's advent into society. It was the high-flying brent who, knowing how the sensitive girl, made keenly conscious at every turn of her defective training and ingenuous ignorance, had often watched their evening flight with longing gaze, now 'houked' dismally at the recollection. It was at this hour and season that the usual vague lamentings of Dedlow Marsh seemed to find at last a preordained expression. And it was at such a time, when light and water were both fading, and the blackness of the Marsh was once more reasserting itself, that a small boat was creeping along one of the tortuous inlets, at times half hiding behind the bank like a wounded bird. As it slowly penetrated inland it seemed to be impelled by its solitary occupant in a hesitating uncertain way, as if to escape observation rather than as if directed to any positive bourn. Stopping beside a bank of reeds at last, the figure rose stoopingly, and drew a gun from between its feet and the bottom of the boat. As the light fell upon its face, it could be seen that it was James Culpepper! James Culpepper! hardly recognisable in the swollen features, bloodshot eyes, and tremulous hands of that ruined figure! James Culpepper, only retaining a single trace of his former self in his look of set and passionate purpose! And that purpose was to kill himself—to be found dead, as his father had been before him—in an open boat, adrift upon the Marsh!

It was not the outcome of a sudden fancy. The idea had first come to him in a taunting allusion from the drunken lips of one of his ruder companions, for which he had stricken the offender to the earth. It had since haunted his waking hours of remorse and hopeless fatuity; it had seemed to be the one relief and atonement he could make his devoted sister, and, more fatuous than all, it seemed to the miserable boy the one revenge he would take upon the faithless coquette, who for a year had played with his simplicity, and had helped to drive him to the distraction of cards and drink.

Only that morning Colonel Preston had forbidden him the house; and now it seemed to him the end had come. He raised his distorted face above the reedy bank for a last tremulous and half-frightened glance at the landscape he was leaving for ever. A glint in the western sky lit up the front of his deserted dwelling in the distance, abreast of which the windings of the inlet had unwittingly led him. As he looked he started, and involuntarily dropped into a crouching attitude. For, to his superstitious terror, the sealed windows of his old home were open, the bright panes were glittering with the fading light, and on the outer gallery the familiar figure of his sister stood, as of old, awaiting his return! Was he really going mad, or had this last vision of his former youth been purposely vouchsafed him?

But, even as he gazed, the appearance of another figure in the landscape beyond the house proved the reality of his vision, and as suddenly distracted him from all else. For it was the apparition of a man on horseback approaching the house from the upland; and even at that distance he recognised its well-known outlines. It was Calvert! Calvert the traitor! Calvert, the man whom he had long suspected as being the secret lover and destined husband of Cicely Preston! Calvert, who had deceived him with his calm equanimity and his affected preference for Maggie, to conceal his deliberate understanding with Cicely. What was he doing here? Was he a double traitor, and now trying to deceive *her* — as he had him? And Maggie here! This sudden return — this preconcerted meeting. It was infamy!

For a moment he remained stupefied, and then, with a mechanical instinct, plunged his head and face in the lazy-flowing water, and then once again rose cool and collected. The half-mad distraction of his previous resolve had given way to another, more deliberate, but not less desperate determination. He knew now *why* he came there — *why* he had brought his gun — why his boat had stopped when it did!

Lying flat in the bottom, he tore away fragments of the crumbling bank to fill his frail craft, until he had sunk it to the gunwale, and below the low level of the Marsh. Then, using his hands as noiseless paddles, he propelled this rude imitation of a floating log slowly past the line of vision, until the tongue of bushes had hidden him from view. With a rapid glance at the darkening flat, he then seized his gun, and springing to the spongy bank, half crouching half crawling through reeds and tussocks, he made his way to the brush. A foot and eye less experienced would have plunged its owner helpless in the black quagmire. At one edge of the thicket he heard hoofs trampling the dried twigs. Calvert's horse was already there, tied to a skirting alder.

He ran to the house, but, instead of attracting attention by ascending the creaking steps, made his way to the piles below the rear gallery and climbed to it noiselessly. It was the spot where the deserter had ascended a year ago, and, like him, he could see and hear all that passed distinctly. Calvert stood near the open door as if departing. Maggie stood between him and the window, her face in shadow, her hands clasped tightly behind her. A profound sadness, partly of the dying day and waning light, and partly of some vague expiration of their own sorrow, seemed to encompass them. Without knowing why, a strange trembling took the place of James Culpepper's fierce determination, and a film of moisture stole across his staring eyes.

'When I tell you that I believe all this will pass, and that you will still win your brother back to you,' said Calvert's sad but clear voice, 'I will tell you why—although, perhaps, it is only a part of that confidence you command me to withhold. When I first saw you, I, myself, had fallen into like dissolute habits; less excusable than him, for I had some experience of the world and its follies. When I met *you*, and fell under the influence of your pure, simple, and healthy life; when I saw that isolation, monotony misunderstanding, even the sense of superiority to one's surroundings could be lived down and triumphed over, without vulgar distractions or pitiful ambitions; when I learned to love you —hear me out, Miss Culpepper, I beg you— you saved *me*—I, who was nothing to you, even as I honestly believe you will still save your brother, whom you love.'

'How do you know I didn't *ruin* him?' she said, turning upon him bitterly. 'How do you know that it wasn't to get rid of *our* monotony, *our* solitude, that I drove him to this vulgar distraction, this pitiful—yes, you were right—pitiful ambition?'

'Because it isn't your real nature,' he said quietly.

'My real nature,' she repeated with a half-savage vehemence that seemed to be goaded from her by his very gentleness, 'my real nature! What did *he*—what do *you* know of it?—My real nature!—I'll tell you what it was,' she went on passionately. 'It was to be revenged on you all for your cruelty, your heartlessness, your wickedness to me and mine in the past. It was to pay you off for your slanders of my dead father—for the selfishness that left me and Jim alone with his dead body on the Marsh. That was what sent me to Logport—to get even with you—to—to fool and flaunt you! There, you have it now! And now that God has punished me for it by crushing my brother—you—you expect me to let you crush *me* too.'

'But,' he said eagerly, advancing towards her, 'you are wronging me—you are wronging yourself, cruelly.'

'Stop,' she said, stepping back, with her hands still locked behind her. 'Stay where you are. There! That's enough!' She drew herself up and let her hands fall at her side. 'Now, let us speak of Jim,' she said coldly.

Without seeming to hear her, he regarded her for the first time with hopeless sadness.

'Why did you let my brother believe you were his rival with Cicely Preston?' she asked impatiently.

'Because I could not undeceive him without

telling him I hopelessly loved his sister. You are proud, Miss Culpepper,' he said, with the first tinge of bitterness in his even voice. 'Can you not understand that others may be proud too?'

'No,' she said bluntly; 'it is not pride but weakness. You could have told him what you knew to be true. That there could be nothing in common between her folk and such savages as we—that there was a gulf as wide as that Marsh and as black between our natures, our training and theirs, and even if they came to us across it, now and then, to suit their pleasure light and easy as that tide—it was still there to some day ground and swamp them! And if he doubted it, you had only to tell him your own story. You had only to tell him what you have just told me—that you yourself, an officer and a gentleman, thought you loved me—a vulgar, uneducated, savage girl, and that I, kinder to you than you to me or him, made you take it back across that tide, because I couldn't let you link your life with me, and drag you in the mire.'

'You need not have said that, Miss Culpepper,' returned Calvert with the same gentle smile, 'to prove that I am your inferior in all but one thing.'

'And that?' she said quickly.

'Is my love.'

His gentle face was as set now as her own as he moved back slowly towards the door There he paused.

'You tell me to speak of Jim, and Jim only.

Then hear me. I believe that Miss Preston cares for him as far as lies in her young and giddy nature. I could not, therefore, have crushed *his* hope without deceiving him, for there are as cruel deceits prompted by what we call reason as by our love. If you think that a knowledge of this plain truth would help to save him, I beg you to be kinder to him than you have been to me. Or even, let me dare to hope, to *yourself*.'

He slowly crossed the threshold, still holding his cap lightly in his hand.

'When I tell you that I am going away to-morrow on a leave of absence, and that in all probability we may not meet again, you will not misunderstand why I add my prayer to the message your friends in Logport charged me with.

They beg that you will give up your idea of returning here, and come back to them. Believe me, you have made yourself loved and respected there in spite—I beg pardon—perhaps I should say *because* of your pride. Good-night and good-bye.'

For a single instant she turned her set face to the window with a sudden convulsive movement as if she would have called him back, but at the same moment the opposite door creaked and her brother slipped into the room. Whether a quick memory of the deserter's entrance at that door a year ago had crossed her mind, whether there was some strange suggestion in his mud-stained garments and weak deprecating smile, or whether it was the outcome of some desperate struggle within her, there was that in her face that changed his smile into a frightened cry for pardon, as he ran and fell on his knees at her feet. But even as he did so her stern look vanished, and with her arm around him she bent over him and mingled her tears with his.

'I heard it all, Mag, dearest! All! Forgive me! I have been crazy!—wild!—I will reform!—I will be better! I will never disgrace you again, Mag! Never, never! I swear it!'

She reached down and kissed him. After a pause, a weak boyish smile struggled into his face.

'You heard what he said of *her*, Mag. Do you think it might be true?'

She lifted the damp curls from his forehead with a sad half-maternal smile, but did not reply.

'And Mag, dear, don't you think *you* were a

little—just a little—hard on *him?* No! Don't look at me that way, for God's sake! There, I didn't mean anything. Of course you knew best. There, Maggie, dear, look up. Hark there! Listen, Mag, do!'

They lifted their eyes to the dim distance seen through the open door. Borne on the fading light, and seeming to fall and die with it over marsh and river, came the last notes of the bugle from the Fort.

'There! Don't you remember what you used to say, Mag?'

The look that had frightened him had quite left her face now.

'Yes,' she smiled, laying her cold cheek beside his softly. 'Oh yes! It was something that came and went, "Like a song"—"Like a song."'

II

A KNIGHT-ERRANT OF THE FOOT-HILLS

A KNIGHT-ERRANT OF THE FOOT-HILLS

I

As Father Felipe slowly toiled up the dusty road towards the Rancho of the Blessed Innocents, he more than once stopped under the shadow of a sycamore to rest his somewhat lazy mule and to compose his own perplexed thoughts by a few snatches from his breviary. For the good *padre* had some reason to be troubled. The invasion of Gentile Americans that followed the gold discovery of three years before had not confined itself to the plains of the Sacramento, but stragglers had already found their way to the Santa Cruz Valley, and the seclusion of even the mission itself was threatened. It was true that they had not brought their heathen engines to disembowel the earth in search of gold, but it was rumoured that they had already speculated upon the agricultural productiveness of the land, and had espied 'the fatness thereof.' As he reached the higher plateau he could see the afteronon sea-fog—presently to obliterate the fair prospect—already pulling through the gaps in the coast range, and on a nearer slope—no less ominously—the smoke of a recent but more permanently destructive Yankee saw-mill was slowly drifting towards the valley.

'Get up, beast!' said the father, digging his heels into the comfortable flanks of his mule with some human impatience, 'or art *thou*, too, a lazy renegade? Thinkest thou, besotted one, that the heretic will spare thee more work than the Holy Church?'

The mule, thus apostrophised in ear and flesh, shook its head obstinately as if the question was by no means clear to its mind, but nevertheless started into a little trot, which presently brought it to the low *adobe* wall of the courtyard of 'The Innocents,' and entered the gate. A few lounging *peons* in the shadow of an archway took off their broad-brimmed hats and made way for the padre, and a half dozen equally listless *vaqueros* helped him to alight. Accustomed as he was to the indolence and superfluity of his host's retainers, to-day it nevertheless seemed to strike some note of irritation in his breast.

A stout middle-aged woman of ungirt waist and beshawled head and shoulders appeared at the gateway as if awaiting him. After a formal salutation she drew him aside into an inner passage.

'He is away again, your Reverence,' she said.

'Ah—always the same?'

'Yes, your Reverence—and this time to a "meeting" of the heretics at their *pueblo*, at Jonesville—where they will ask him of his land for a road.'

'At a *meeting*?' echoed the priest uneasily.

'Ah yes! a meeting—where Tiburcio says they shout and spit on the ground, your Reverence, and only one has a chair and him they call a " chairman " because of it, and yet he sits not but shouts and spits even as the others and keeps up a tapping with a hammer like a very *pico*. And there it is they are ever " resolving " that which is not, and consider it even as done.'

'Then he is still the same,' said the priest gloomily as the woman paused for breath.

'Only more so, your Reverence, for he reads nought but the newspaper of the *Americanos* that is brought in the ship, the *New York 'errald*—and recites to himself the orations of their legislators. Ah! it was an evil day when the shipwrecked American sailor taught him his uncouth tongue, which, as your Reverence knows, is only fit for beasts and heathen incantation.'

'Pray Heaven *that* were all he learned of him,' said the priest hastily, 'for I have great fear that this sailor was little better than an atheist and an emissary from Satan. But where are these newspapers and the fantasies of *publicita* that fill his mind? I would see them, my daughter.'

'You shall, your Reverence, and more too,' she replied eagerly, leading the way along the passage to a grated door which opened upon a small cell-like apartment whose scant light and less air came through the deeply embayed windows in the outer wall. 'Here is his *estudio*.'

In spite of this open invitation, the padre entered with that air of furtive and minute inspection common to his order. His glance fell upon a rude surveyor's plan of the adjacent embryo town of Jonesville hanging on the wall, which he contemplated with a cold disfavour that even included the highly coloured vignette of the projected Jonesville Hotel in the left-hand corner. He then passed to a supervisor's notice hanging near it, which he examined with a suspicion heightened by that uneasiness common to mere worldly humanity when opposed to an unknown and unfamiliar language. But an exclamation broke from his lips when he confronted an election placard immediately below it. It was printed in Spanish and English, and Father Felipe had no difficulty in reading the announcement that 'Don José Sepulvida would preside at a meeting of the Board of Education in Jonesville as one of the trustees.'

'This is madness,' said the padre.

Observing that Dona Maria was at the moment preoccupied in examining the pictorial pages of an illustrated American weekly which had hitherto escaped his eyes, he took it gently from her hand.

'Pardon, your Reverence,' she said with slightly acidulous deprecation, 'but thanks to the Blessed Virgin and your Reverence's teaching, the text is but gibberish to me and I did but glance at the pictures.'

'Much evil may come in with the eye,' said the priest sententiously, 'as I will presently show thee. We have here,' he continued, pointing to an illustration of certain college athletic sports, 'a number of youthful cavaliers posturing and capering in a partly nude condition before a number of shameless women, who emulate the saturnalia of heathen Rome by waving their handkerchiefs. We have here a companion picture,' he said, indicating an illustration of gymnastic exercises by the students of a female academy at 'Commencement,' 'in which, as thou seest, even the aged of both sexes unblushingly assist as spectators with every expression of immodest satisfaction.'

'Have they no bull-fights or other seemly recreation that they must indulge in such wantonness?' asked Dona Maria indignantly, gazing, however, somewhat curiously at the baleful representations.

'Of all that, my daughter, has their pampered civilisation long since wearied,' returned the good padre, 'for see, this is what they consider a moral and even a religious ceremony.' He turned to an illustration of a woman's rights convention; 'observe with what rapt attention the audience of that heathen temple watch the inspired ravings of that elderly priestess on the daïs. It is even this kind of sacrilegious performance that I am told thy nephew Don José expounds and defends.'

'May the blessed saints preserve us; where will it lead to?' murmured the horrified Dona Maria.

'I will show thee,' said Father Felipe, briskly turning the pages with the same lofty ignoring of the text until he came to a representation of a labour procession. 'There is one of their periodic revolutions unhappily not unknown even in Mexico. Thou perceivest those complacent artisans marching with implements of their craft, accompanied by the military, in the presence of their own stricken masters. Here we see only another instance of the instability of all communities that are not founded on the principles of the Holy Church.'

' And what is to be done with my nephew ? '

The good father's brow darkened with the gloomy religious zeal of two centuries ago. ' We must have a council of the family, the alcalde, and the archbishop, at *once*,' he said ominously. To the mere heretical observer the conclusion might have seemed lame and impotent, but it was as near the Holy Inquisition as the year of grace 1852 could offer.

A few days after this colloquy the unsuspecting subject of it, Don José Sepulvida, was sitting alone in the same apartment. The fading glow of the western sky, through the deep embrasured windows, lit up his rapt and meditative face.

He was a young man of apparently twenty-five, with a colourless satin complexion, dark eyes alternating between melancholy and restless energy, a narrow high forehead, long straight hair, and a lightly pencilled moustache. He was said to resemble the well-known portrait of the Marquis of Monterey in the mission church, a face that was alleged to leave a deep and lasting impression upon the observers. It was undoubtedly owing to this quality during a brief visit of the famous viceroy to a remote and married ancestress of Don José at Leon that the singular resemblance may be attributed.

A heavy and hesitating step along the passage stopped before the grating. Looking up, Don José beheld to his astonishment the slightly inflamed face of Roberto, a vagabond

American whom he had lately taken into his employment.

Roberto, a polite translation of 'Bob the Bucker,' cleaned out at a monte-bank in Santa Cruz, penniless and profligate, had sold his mustang to Don José and recklessly thrown himself in with the bargain. Touched by the rascal's extravagance, the quality of the mare, and observing that Bob's habits had not yet affected his seat in the saddle, but rather lent a demoniac vigour to his chase of wild cattle, Don José had retained rider and horse in his service as vaquero.

Bucking Bob, observing that his employer was alone, coolly opened the door without ceremony, shut it softly behind him, and then closed the wooden shutter of the grating. Don José surveyed him with mild surprise and dignified composure. The man appeared perfectly sober, —it was a peculiarity of his dissipated habits that, when not actually raving with drink, he was singularly shrewd and practical.

'Look yer, Don Kosay,' he began in a brusque but guarded voice, 'you and me is pards. When ye picked me and the mare up and set us on our legs again in this yer ranch, I allowed I'd tie to ye whenever you was in trouble—and wanted me. And I reckon that's what's the matter now. For from what I see and hear on every side, although you're the boss of this consarn, you're surrounded by a gang of spies and traitors. Your comings and goings, your ins and outs, is dogged and followed and blown upon. The folks you trust is playing it on ye, It ain't for me to say why or wherefore—what's their rights and what's yourn—but I've come to tell ye that if you don't get up and get outer this ranch them d——d priests and your own flesh and blood—your aunts and your uncles and your cousins, will have you chucked outer your property, and run into a lunatic asylum.'

'Me—Don José Sepulvida—a lunatico! You are yourself crazy of drink, friend Roberto.'

'Yes,' said Roberto grimly, 'but that kind ain't *illegal*, while your makin' ducks and drakes of your property and going into 'Merikin ideas and 'Merikin speculations they reckon is. And speakin' on the square, it ain't *nat'ral*.'

Don José sprang to his feet and began to pace up and down his cell-like study. 'Ah, I remember now,' he muttered, 'I begin to comprehend: Father Felipe's homilies and discourses!

My aunt's too affectionate care! My cousin's discreet consideration! The prompt attention of my servants! I see it all! And you,' he said, suddenly facing Roberto, 'why come you to tell me this?'

'Well, boss,' said the American drily, 'I reckoned to stand by you.'

'Ah,' said Don José, visibly affected, 'Good Roberto, come hither, child, you may kiss my hand.'

'If! it's all the same to you, Don Kosay,—*that* kin slide.'

'Ah, if—yes,' said Don José, meditatively putting his hand to his forehead, 'miserable that I am!—I remembered not you were *Americano*. Pardon, my friend—embrace me—*Conpañero y Amigo.*'

With characteristic gravity he reclined for a moment upon Robert's astonished breast. Then recovering himself with equal gravity he paused, lifted his hand with gentle warning, marched to a recess in the corner, unhooked a rapier hanging from the wall and turned to his companion—

'We will defend ourselves, friend Roberto. It is the sword of the *Comandante*—my ancestor. The blade is of Toledo.'

'An ordinary six-shooter of Colt's would lay over that,' said Roberto grimly—'but that ain't your game just now, Don Kosay. You must get up and get, and at once. You must *vamose* the ranch afore they lay hold of you and have you up before the alcalde. Once away from here, they daren't follow you where there's 'Merikin law, and when you kin fight 'em on the square.'

'Good,' said Don José with melancholy preciseness. 'You are wise, friend Roberto. We may fight them later as you say—on the square, or in the open Plaza. And you, *camarado, you* shall go with me—you and your mare.'

Sincere as the American had been in his offer of service, he was somewhat staggered at this imperative command. But only for a moment. 'Well,' he said lazily, 'I don't care if I do.'

'But,' said Don José with increased gravity, 'you *shall* care, friend Roberto. We shall make an alliance, an union. It is true, my brother, you drink of whisky, and at such times are even as a madman. It has been recounted to me that it was necessary to your existence that you are a lunatic three days of the week. Who knows?

I myself, though I drink not of *aguardiente*, am accused of fantasies for all time. Necessary it becomes therefore that we should go *together*. My fantasies and speculations cannot injure you, my brother; your whisky shall not empoison me. We shall go together in the great world of your American ideas of which I am much inflamed. We shall together breathe as one the spirit of Progress and Liberty. We shall be even as neophytes making of ourselves Apostles of Truth. I absolve and renounce myself henceforth of my family. I shall take to myself the sister and the brother, the aunt and the uncle, as we proceed. I devote myself to humanity alone. I devote *you*, my friend, and the mare — though happily she has not a Christian soul — to this glorious mission.'

The few level last rays of light lit up a faint enthusiasm in the face of Don José, but without altering his imperturbable gravity. The *vaquero* eyed him curiously and half doubtfully.

'We will go to-morrow,' resumed Don José with solemn decision, 'for it is Wednesday. It was a Sunday that thou didst ride the mare up the steps of the Fonda and demanded that thy liquor should be served to thee in a pail. I remember it, for the landlord of the Fonda claimed twenty *pesos* for damage and the kissing of his wife. Therefore by computation, good Roberto, thou shouldst be sober until Friday, and we shall have two clear days to fly before thy madness again seizes thee.'

'They kin say what they like, Don Kosay, but *your* head is level,' returned the unabashed

American, grasping Don José's hand. 'All right, then. *Hasta mañana,* as your folks say.'

'Hasta mañana,' repeated Don José gravely.

At daybreak next morning, while slumber still weighted the lazy eyelids of 'the Blessed Innocents,' Don José Sepulvida and his trusty squire Roberto, otherwise known as 'Bucking Bob,' rode forth unnoticed from the corral.

II

THREE days had passed. At the close of the third, Don José was seated in a cosy private apartment of the San Mateo Hotel, where they had halted for an arranged interview with his lawyer before reaching San Francisco. From his window he could see the surrounding park-like avenues of oaks and the level white high road, now and then clouded with the dust of passing teams. But his eyes were persistently fixed upon a small copy of the American Constitution before him. Suddenly there was a quick rap on his door, and before he could reply to it a man brusquely entered.

Don José raised his head slowly, and recognised the landlord. But the intruder, apparently awed by the gentle, grave, and studious figure before him, fell back for an instant in an attitude of surly apology.

'Enter freely, my good Jenkinson,' said Don José, with a quiet courtesy that had all the effect of irony. 'The apartment, such as it is, is at your disposition. It is even yours as is the house.'

'Well, I'm darned if I know as it is,' said the landlord, recovering himself roughly, 'and that's jest what's the matter. Yer's that man of yours smashing things right and left in the bar-room and chuckin' my waiters through the window.'

'Softly, softly, good Jenkinson,' said Don

José, putting a mark in the pages of the volume before him. 'It is necessary first that I should correct your speech. He is not my "*man*," which I comprehend to mean a slave, a hireling, a thing obnoxious to the great American nation which *I* admire and to which *he* belongs. Therefore, good Jenkinson, say "friend," "companion," "guide," "philosopher," if you will. As to the rest, it is of no doubt as you relate. I myself have heard the breakings of glass and small dishes as I sit here: three times I have seen your waiters projected into the road with much violence and confusion. To myself I have then said, even as I say to you, good Jenkinson, "Patience, patience, the end is not far." In four hours,' continued Don José, holding up four fingers, 'he shall make a finish. Until then, not.'

'Well, I'm d——d,' ejaculated Jenkinson, gasping for breath in his indignation.

'Nay, excellent Jenkinson, not dam-ned but of a possibility dam-*aged*. That I shall repay when he have make a finish.'

'But, darn it all,' broke in the landlord angrily.

'Ah,' said Don José gravely, 'you would be paid before! Good; for how much shall you value *all* you have in your bar?'

Don José's imperturbability evidently shook the landlord's faith in the soundness of his own position. He looked at his guest critically and audaciously.

'It cost me two hundred dollars to fit it up,' he said curtly.

Don José rose, and, taking a buckskin purse

from his saddle bag, counted out four slugs[1] and handed them to the stupefied Jenkinson. The next moment, however, his host recovered himself, and casting the slugs back on the little table, brought his fist down with an emphasis that made them dance.

'But, look yer—suppose I want this thing stopped—you hear me—*stopped*—now.'

'That would be interfering with the liberty of the subject, my good Jenkinson—which God forbid!' said Don José calmly. 'Moreover, it is the custom of the *Americanos*—a habit of my friend Roberto — a necessity of his existence —and so recognised of his friends. Patience and courage, Señor Jenkinson. Stay — ah, I

---

[1] Hexagonal gold pieces valued at $50 each, issued by a private firm as coin in the early days.

comprehend! you have — of a possibility — a wife?'

'No, I'm a widower,' said Jenkinson sharply.

'Then I congratulate you. My friend Roberto would have kissed her. It is also of his habit. Truly you have escaped much. I embrace you, Jenkinson.'

He threw his arms gravely around Jenkinson, in whose astounded face at last an expression of dry humour faintly dawned. After a moment's survey of Don José's impenetrable gravity, he coolly gathered up the gold coins, and saying that he would assess the damages and return the difference, he left the room as abruptly as he had entered it.

But Don José was not destined to remain long in peaceful study of the American Constitution. He had barely taken up the book again and renewed his serious contemplation of its excellencies when there was another knock at his door. This time, in obedience to his invitation to enter, the new visitor approached with more deliberation and a certain formality.

He was a young man of apparently the same age as Don José, handsomely dressed, and of a quiet self-possession and gravity almost equal to his host's.

'I believe I am addressing Don José Sepulvida,' he said with a familiar yet courteous inclination of his handsome head. Don José, who had risen in marked contrast to his reception of his former guest, answered—

'You are truly making to him a great honour.'

'Well, you're going it blind as far as *I'm* concerned certainly,' said the young man, with a slight smile, 'for you don't know *me*.'

'Pardon, my friend,' said Don José gently, 'in this book, this great Testament of your glorious nation, I have read that you are all equal, one not above, one not below the other, I salute in you, the Nation! It is enough!'

'Thank you,' returned the stranger, with a face that, saving the faintest twinkle in the corner of his dark eyes, was immovable as his host's, 'but for the purposes of my business I had better say I am Jack Hamlin, a gambler, and am just now dealing faro in the Florida saloon round the corner.'

He paused carelessly, as if to allow Don José

the protest he did not make, and then continued—

'The matter is this. One of your *vaqueros*, who is, however, an American, was round there an hour ago bucking against faro, and put up and *lost*, not only the mare he was riding, but a horse which I have just learned is yours. Now we reckon, over there, that we can make enough money playing a square game, without being obliged to take property from a howling drunkard, to say nothing of it not belonging to him, and I've come here, Don José, to say that if you'll send over and bring away your man and your horse you can have 'em both.'

'If I have comprehend, honest Hamlin,' said Don José slowly, 'this Roberto, who was my *vaquero* and is my brother, has approached this faro game by himself, unsolicited?'

'He certainly didn't seem shy of it,' said Mr. Hamlin with equal gravity. 'To the best of my knowledge, he looked as if he'd been there before.'

'And if he had won, excellent Hamlin, you would have given him the equal of his mare and horse?'

'A hundred dollars for each, yes, certainly.'

'Then I see not why I should send for the property which is truly no longer mine, nor for my brother who will amuse himself after the fashion of his country in the company of so honourable a *caballero* as yourself? Stay! oh imbecile that I am. I have not remembered. You would possibly say that he has no longer of horses? Play him; play him, admirable yet prudent Hamlin. *I* have two thousand horses! Of a surety he cannot exhaust them in four hours. Therefore play him, trust to me for *recompensa*, and have no fear.'

A quick flush covered the stranger's cheek, and his eyebrows momentarily contracted. He walked carelessly to the window, however, glanced out, and then turned to Don José.

'May I ask, then,' he said with almost sepulchral gravity, 'is anybody taking care of you?'

'Truly,' returned Don José cautiously, 'there is my brother and friend Roberto.'

'Ah! Roberto, certainly,' said Mr. Hamlin profoundly.

'Why do you ask, considerate friend?'

'Oh! I only thought, with your kind of opinions, you must often feel lonely in California. Good-bye. He shook Don José's hand heartily, took up his hat, inclined his head with graceful seriousness, and passed out of the room. In the hall he met the landlord.

'Well,' said Jenkinson, with a smile half anxious half insinuating, ' you saw him? What do you think of him?'

Mr. Hamlin paused and regarded Jenkinson with a calmly contemplative air, as if he were trying to remember first who he was, and secondly why he should speak to him at all. 'Think of whom?' he repeated carelessly.

'Why him—you know—Don José.'

'I did not see anything the matter with him,' returned Hamlin with frigid simplicity.

'What? nothing queer?'

'Well, no—except that he's a guest in *your* house,' said Hamlin with great cheerfulness. 'But then, as you keep a hotel, you can't help occasionally admitting a—gentleman.'

Mr. Jenkinson smiled the uneasy smile of a man who knew that his interlocutor's playfulness occasionally extended to the use of a derringer, in which he was singularly prompt and proficient, and Mr. Hamlin, equally conscious of that knowledge on the part of his companion, descended the staircase composedly.

But the day had darkened gradually into night, and Don José was at last compelled to put aside his volume. The sound of a large bell rung violently along the hall and passages admonished him that the American dinner was ready, and although the viands and the mode of cooking were not entirely to his fancy, he had, in his grave enthusiasm for the national habits, attended the *table d'hôte* regularly with Roberto. On reaching the lower hall he was informed that his henchman had early succumbed to the potency of his libations, and had already been carried by two men to bed. Receiving this information with his usual stoical composure, he entered the dining-room, but was surprised to find that a separate table had been prepared for him by the landlord, and that a rude attempt had been made to serve him with his own native dishes.

'Señores y Señoritos,' said Don José, turning from it and with grave politeness addressing the assembled company, 'if I seem to-day to partake alone and in a reserved fashion of certain viands that have been prepared for me, it is truly from no lack of courtesy to your distinguished company, but rather, I protest, to avoid the appearance of greater discourtesy to our excellent Jenkinson, who has taken some pains and trouble to comport his establishment to what he conceives to be my desires. Wherefore, my friends, in God's name fall to, the same as if I were not present, and grace be with you.

A few stared at the tall, gentle, melancholy figure with some astonishment; a few whispered to their neighbours, but when, at the conclusion of his repast, Don José arose and again saluted the company, one or two stood up and smilingly returned the courtesy, and Polly Jenkinson, the landlord's youngest daughter, to the great delight of her companions, blew him a kiss.

After visiting the *vaquero* in his room, and with his own hand applying some native ointment to the various contusions and scratches which recorded the late engagements of the unconscious Roberto, Don José placed a gold coin in the hands of the Irish chambermaid, and bidding her look after the sleeper, he threw his *serape* over his shoulders and passed into the road. The loungers on the verandah gazed at him curiously, yet half acknowledged his usual serious salutation, and made way for him with a certain respect. Avoiding the few narrow streets of the little town, he pursued his way meditatively along the high road, returning to the hotel after an hour's ramble, as the evening stage-coach had deposited its passengers and departed.

'There's a lady waiting to see you upstairs,' said the landlord with a peculiar smile. 'She rather allowed it wasn't the proper thing to see you alone, or she wasn't quite ekal to it, I reckon, for she got my Polly to stand by her.'

'Your Polly, good Jenkinson? said Don José interrogatively.

'My darter, Don José.'

'Ah, truly! I am twice blessed,' said Don José, gravely ascending the staircase.

On entering the room he perceived a tall large-featured woman with an extraordinary quantity of blonde hair parted on one side of her broad forehead, sitting upon the sofa. Beside her sat Polly Jenkinson, her fresh, honest, and rather pretty face beaming with delighted expectation and mischief. Don José saluted them with a formal courtesy which, however, had no trace of the fact that he really did not remember anything of them.

'I called,' said the large-featured woman with a voice equally pronounced, 'in reference to a request from you, which, though perhaps unconventional in the extreme, I have been able to meet by the intervention of this young lady's company. My name on this card may not be familiar to you—but I am "Dorothy Dewdrop."'

A slight movement of abstraction and surprise passed over Don José's face, but as quickly vanished as he advanced towards her and gracefully raised the tips of her fingers to his lips. 'Have I then, at last, the privilege of beholding that most distressed and deeply injured of women! Or is it but a dream!'

It certainly was not, as far as concerned the substantial person of the woman before him, who, however, seemed somewhat uneasy under his words as well as the demure scrutiny of Miss Jenkinson. 'I thought you might have forgotten,' she said with slight acerbity, 'that you desired an interview with the authoress of——'

'Pardon,' interrupted Don José, standing before her in an attitude of the deepest sympathising dejection, 'I had not forgotten. It is now three weeks since I have read in the journal *Golden Gate* the eloquent and touching poem of your sufferings, and your aspirations, and your miscomprehensions by those you love.

I remember as yesterday that you have said, that cruel fate have linked you to a soulless state—that—but I speak not well your own beautiful language—you are in tears at evenfall "because that you are not understood of others, and that your soul recoiled from iron bonds, until, as in a dream, you sought succour and release in some true Knight of equal plight."'

'I am told,' said the large-featured woman with some satisfaction, 'that the poem to which you allude has been generally admired.'

'Admired! Señora,' said Don José, with still darker sympathy, 'it is not the word; it is *felt*. I have felt it. When I read those words of distress, I am touched of compassion! I have said, This woman, so disconsolate, so oppressed, must be relieved, protected! I have wrote to you, at the *Golden Gate*, to see me here.'

'And I have come, as you perceive,' said the poetess, rising with a slight smile of constraint; 'and, emboldened by your appreciation, I have brought a few trifles thrown off——'

'Pardon, unhappy Señora,' interrupted Don José, lifting his hand deprecatingly without relaxing his melancholy precision, 'but to a cavalier further evidence is not required—and I have not yet make finish. I have not content myself to *write* to you. I have sent my trusty friend Roberto to inquire at the *Golden Gate* of your condition. I have found there, most unhappy and persecuted friend—that with truly angelic forbearance, you have not told *all*—that you are *married*, and that of a necessity it is your husband that is cold and soulless and unsympathising—and all that you describe.'

'Sir!' said the poetess, rising in angry consternation.

'I have written to him,' continued Don José, with unheeding gravity; 'have appealed to him as a friend, I have conjured him as a *caballero*, I have threatened him even as a champion of the Right, I have said to him, in effect—that this must not be as it is. I have informed him that I have made an appointment with you even at this house, and I challenged him to meet you here—in this room—even at this instant, and, with God's help, we should make good our charges against him. It is yet early; I have allowed time for the lateness of the stage and the fact that he will come by another conveyance. Therefore, oh Doña Dewdrop, tremble not like thy namesake as it were on the leaf of apprehension and expectancy. I, Don José, am here to protect thee. I will take these charges'—gently withdrawing the manuscripts from her astonished grasp—'though even, as I related to thee before, I want them not, yet we will together confront him with them and make them good against him.'

'Are you mad?' demanded the lady in almost stentorian accents, 'or is this an unmanly hoax?' Suddenly she stopped in undeniable consternation. 'Good heavens,' she muttered, 'if Abner should believe this. He is *such* a fool! He has lately been queer and jealous. Oh dear!' she said, turning to Polly Jenkinson with the first indication of feminine weakness, '*is* he telling the truth? is he crazy? what shall I do?'

Polly Jenkinson, who had witnessed the interview with the intensest enjoyment, now rose equal to the occasion.

'You have made a mistake,' she said, uplifting her demure blue eyes to Don José's dark and melancholy gaze. 'This lady is a *poetess!* The sufferings she depicts, the sorrows she feels, are in the *imagination*, in her fancy only.'

'Ah!' said Don José gloomily, 'then it is all false.'

'No,' said Polly quickly, 'only they are not her *own*, you know. They are somebody else's. She only describes them for another, don't you see?'

'And who then is this unhappy one?' asked the Don quickly.

'Well—a—friend,' stammered Polly hesitatingly.

'A friend!' repeated Don José. 'Ah, I see, of possibility a dear one, even,' he continued, gazing with tender melancholy into the untroubled cerulean depths of Polly's eyes, 'even, but no, child, it could not be! *thou* art too young.'

'Ah,' said Polly, with an extraordinary gulp and a fierce nudge of the poetess, 'but it *was* me.

'You, Señorita,' repeated Don José, falling back in an attitude of mingled admiration and pity. 'You, the child of Jenkinson!'

'Yes, yes,' joined in the poetess hurriedly, 'but that isn't going to stop the consequences of your wretched blunder. My husband will be furious, and will be here at any moment. Good gracious! what is that?'

The violent slamming of a distant door at that instant, the sounds of quick scuffling on the staircase, and the uplifting of an irate voice had reached her ears and thrown her back in the arms of Polly Jenkinson. Even the young girl herself turned an anxious gaze towards the door. Don José alone was unmoved.

'Possess yourselves in peace, Señoritas,' he said calmly. 'We have here only the characteristic convalescence of my friend and brother, the excellent Roberto. He will ever recover himself from drink with violence, even as he precipitates himself into it with fury. He has been prematurely awakened. I will discover the cause.'

With an elaborate bow to the frightened women, he left the room. Scarcely had the door closed when the poetess turned quickly to Polly. 'The man's a stark staring lunatic, but, thank Heaven, Abner will see it at once. And now let's get away while we can. To think,' she said, snatching up her scattered manuscripts, 'that *that* was all the beast wanted.'

'I'm sure he's very gentle and kind,' said Polly, recovering her dimples with a demure pout; 'but stop, he's coming back.'

It was indeed Don José re-entering the room with the composure of a relieved and self-satisfied mind. 'It is even as I said, Señora, he began, taking the poetess's hand, 'and *more*. You are *saved!*'

As the women only stared at each other, he gravely folded his arms and continued: 'I will explain. For the instant I have not remember that in imitation of your own delicacy, I have given to your husband in my letter not the name of myself, but, as a mere *Don Fulano*, the name of my brother Roberto— "Bucking Bob." Your husband have this moment arrive! Penetrating the bedroom of the excellent Roberto, he has indiscreetly seize him in his bed, without explanation, without introduction, without fear! The excellent Roberto, ever ready for such distractions, have respond! In a word, to use the language of the good Jenkinson — our host, our father

—who was present, he have "wiped the floor with your husband," and have even carried him down the staircase to the street. Believe me, he will not return. You are free!'

'Fool! Idiot! Crazy beast!' said the poetess, dashing past him and out of the door. 'You shall pay for this!'

Don José did not change his imperturbable and melancholy calm. 'And now, little one,' he said, dropping on one knee before the half-frightened Polly, 'child of Jenkinson, now that thy perhaps too excitable sponsor has, in a poet's caprice, abandoned thee for some newer fantasy, confide in me thy distress, to me, thy Knight, and tell the story of thy sorrows.'

'But,' said Polly, rising to her feet and struggling between a laugh and a cry. 'I haven't any sorrows. Oh dear! don't you see, it's only her *fancy* to make me seem so There's nothing the matter with me.'

'Nothing the matter,' repeated Don José slowly. 'You have no distress? You want no succour, no relief, no protector? This then is but another delusion!' he said, rising sadly.

'Yes, no—that is—oh, my gracious goodness!' said Polly, hopelessly divided between a sense of the ridiculous and some strange attraction in the dark gentle eyes that were fixed upon her half reproachfully. 'You don't understand.'

Don José replied only with a melancholy smile, and then going to the door, opened it with a bowed head and respectful courtesy. At the act, Polly plucked up courage again, and with it a slight dash of her old audacity.

'I'm sure I'm very sorry that I ain't got any love sorrows,' she said demurely. 'And I suppose it's very dreadful in me not to have been raving and broken-hearted over somebody or other as that woman has said. Only,' she waited till she had gained the secure vantage of the threshold, 'I never knew a gentleman to *object* to it before!'

With this Parthian arrow from her blue eyes she slipped into the passage and vanished through the door of the opposite parlour. For an instant Don José remained motionless and reflecting. Then, recovering himself with grave precision, he deliberately picked up his narrow black gloves from the table, drew them on, took his hat in his hand, and solemnly striding across the passage, entered the door that had just closed behind her.

III

It must not be supposed that in the meantime the flight of Don José and his follower was unattended by any commotion at the Rancho of the Blessed Innocents. At the end of three hours' deliberation, in which the retainers were severally examined, the corral searched, and the well in the courtyard sounded, scouts were despatched in different directions, who returned with the surprising information that the fugitives were not in the vicinity. A trustworthy messenger was sent to Monterey for 'custom-house paper,' on which to draw up a formal declaration of the affair. The archbishop was summoned from San Luis, and Don Victor and Don Vincente Sepulvida, with the Doñas Carmen and Inez Alvarado, and a former alcalde gathered at a family council the next day. In this serious conclave the good Father Felipe once more expounded the alienated condition and the dangerous reading of the absent man. In the midst of which the ordinary post brought a letter from Don José, calmly inviting the family to dine with him and Roberto at San Mateo on the following Wednesday. The document was passed gravely from hand to hand. Was it a fresh evidence of mental aberration—an audacity of frenzy—or a trick of the vaquero? The archbishop and alcalde shook their heads—it was without doubt a lawless—even a sacrilegious and blasphemous *fête*. But a certain curiosity of the ladies and of Father Felipe carried the day Without formally accepting the invitation it was decided that the family should examine the afflicted man, with a view of taking active measures hereafter. On the day appointed, the travelling carriage of the Sepulvidas, an equipage coeval with the beginning of the century, drawn by two white mules gaudily caparisoned, halted before the hotel at San Mateo and disgorged Father Felipe, the Donas Carmen and Inez Alvaredo and Maria Sepulvida, while Don Victor and Don Vincente Sepulvida, their attendant cavaliers on fiery mustangs, like outriders, drew rein at the same time. A slight thrill of excitement, as of the advent of a possible circus, had preceded them through the little town, a faint blending of cigarette smoke and garlic announced their presence on the verandah.

Ushered into the parlour of the hotel, apparently set apart for their reception, they were embarrassed at not finding their host present. But they were still more disconcerted when a tall full-bearded stranger, with a shrewd amused-looking face, rose from a chair by the window, and stepping forward, saluted them in fluent Spanish with a slight American accent.

'I have to ask you, gentlemen and ladies,' he began, with a certain insinuating ease and frankness that alternately aroused and lulled their suspicions, 'to pardon the absence of our friend Don José Sepulvida at this preliminary greeting. For to be perfectly frank with you, although the ultimate aim and object of our gathering is a social one, you are doubtless aware that certain infelicities and misunderstandings —common to most families—have occurred, and a free, dispassionate, unprejudiced discussion and disposal of them at the beginning will only tend to augment the goodwill of our gathering.'

'The Señor without doubt is——' suggested the padre, with a polite interrogative pause.

'Pardon me! I forgot to introduce myself. Colonel Parker—entirely at your service and that of these charming ladies.'

The ladies referred to allowed their eyes to rest with evident prepossession on the insinuating stranger. 'Ah, a soldier,' said Don Vincente.

'Formerly,' said the American lightly, 'at present a lawyer, the counsel of Don José.'

A sudden rigour of suspicion stiffened the company; the ladies withdrew their eyes; the priest and the Sepulvidas exchanged glances.

'Come,' said Colonel Parker, with apparent unconsciousness of the effect of his disclosure, 'let us begin frankly. You have, I believe, some anxiety in regard to the mental condition of Don José.'

'We believe him to be mad,' said Padre Felipe promptly, 'irresponsible, possessed!'

'That is your opinion, good,' said the lawyer quietly.

'And ours too,' clamoured the party, 'without doubt.'

'Good,' returned the lawyer with perfect cheerfulness. 'As his relations, you have no doubt had superior opportunities for observing his condition. I understand also that you may think it necessary to have him legally declared *non compos*, a proceeding which, you are aware, might result in the incarceration of our distinguished friend in a mad-house.'

'Pardon, Señor,' interrupted Dona Maria proudly, 'you do not comprehend the family. When a Sepulvida is visited of God we do not ask the Government to confine him like a criminal. We protect him in his own house from the consequences of his frenzy.'

'From the machinations of the worldly and heretical,' broke in the priest, 'and from the waste and dispersion of inherited possessions.'

'Very true,' continued Colonel Parker, with unalterable good humour, 'but I was only about to say that there might be conflicting evidence of his condition. For instance, our friend has been here three days. In that time he has had three interviews with three individuals under singular circumstances.' Colonel Parker then briefly recounted the episodes of the landlord, the gambler, Miss Jenkinson and the poetess as they had been related to him. 'Yet,' he continued, 'all but one of these individuals are willing to swear that they not only believe Don José perfectly sane, but endowed with a singularly sound judgment. In fact, the testimony of Mr. Hamlin and Miss Jenkinson is remarkably clear on that subject.'

The company exchanged a supercilious smile 'Do you not see, oh Señor Advocate,' said Don Vincente compassionately, 'that this is but a conspiracy to avail themselves of our relative's weakness. Of a necessity they find him sane who benefits them.'

'I have thought of that, and am glad to hear you say so,' returned the lawyer still more cheerfully, 'for your prompt opinion emboldens me to be at once perfectly frank with you. Briefly then, Don José has summoned me here to make a final disposition of his property. In the carrying out of certain theories of his, which it is not my province to question, he has resolved upon comparative poverty for himself as best fitted for his purpose, and to employ his wealth solely for others. In fact, of all his vast possessions, he retains for himself only an income sufficient for the bare necessaries of life.'

'And you have done this?' they asked in one voice.

'Not yet,' said the lawyer.

'Blessed San Antonio, we have come in time,' ejaculated Doña Carmen. 'Another day and it would have been too late, it was an inspiration of the Blessed Innocents themselves,' said Doña Maria, crossing herself. 'Can you longer doubt that this is the wildest madness?' said Father Felipe with flashing eyes.

'Yet,' returned the lawyer, caressing his heavy beard with a meditative smile, 'the ingenious fellow actually instanced the vows of *your own order*, reverend sir, as an example in support of his theory. But to be brief. Conceiving then that his holding of property was a mere accident of heritage, not admitted by him, unworthy his acceptance, and a relic of superstitious ignorance——'

'This is the very sacrilege of Satanic prepossession,' broke in the priest indignantly.

'He therefore,' continued the lawyer composedly, 'makes over and reverts the whole of his possessions, with the exceptions I have stated, to his family and the Church.'

A breathless and stupefying silence fell upon the company. In the dead hush the sound of Polly Jenkinson's piano played in a distant room could be distinctly heard. With their vacant eyes staring at him the speaker continued—

'That deed of gift I have drawn up as he dictated it. I don't mind saying that in the opinion of some he might be declared *non compos* upon the evidence of that alone. I need not say how relieved I am to find that your opinion coincides with my own.'

'But,' gasped Father Felipe hurriedly, with a quick glance at the others, 'it does not follow that it will be necessary to resort to these legal measures,—care, counsel, persuasion.'

'The general ministering of kinship—nursing, a woman's care—the instincts of affection,' piped Doña Maria in breathless eagerness.

'Any light social distraction—a harmless flirtation—a possible attachment,' suggested Doña Carmen shyly.

'Change of scene—active exercise—experiences—even as those you have related,' broke in Don Vincente.

'I for one have ever been opposed to *legal* measures,' said Don Victor. 'A mere consultation of friends—in fact a *fête* like this is sufficient.'

'But that would be making it a perfectly sane and gratuitous document, not only glaringly inconsistent with your charges, my good friends, with Don José's attitude towards you and his flight from home, but open to the gravest suspicion in law. In fact its apparent propriety in the face of these facts would imply improper influence.'

The countenances of the company fell. The lawyer's face, however, became still more good-humoured and sympathising. 'The case is simply this. If in the opinion of judge and jury Don José is declared insane, the document is worthless except as a proof of that fact or a possible indication of the undue influence of his relations, which might compel the court to select his guardians and trustees elsewhere than among them.'

'Friend Abogado,' said Father Felipe with extraordinary deliberation, 'the document thou has just described so eloquently convinces me beyond all doubt that Don José is not only perfectly sane but endowed with a singular discretion. I consider it as a delicate and high-spirited intimation to us, his friends and kinsmen, of his unalterable and logically just devotion to his family and religion, whatever may seem to be his poetical and imaginative manner of declaring it. I think there is not one here,' continued the padre, looking around him impressively, 'who is not entirely satisfied of Don José's reason and competency to arrange his own affairs.'

'Entirely,' 'truly,' 'perfectly,' eagerly responded the others with affecting spontaneity.

'Nay, more. To prevent any misconception,

we shall deem it our duty to take every opportunity of making our belief publicly known,' added Father Felipe.

The Padre and Colonel Parker gazed long and gravely into each other's eyes. It may have been an innocent touch of the sunlight through the window, but a faint gleam seemed to steal into the pupil of the affable lawyer at the same moment that, probably from the like cause, there was a slight nervous contraction of the left eyelid of the pious father. But it passed and the next instant the door opened to admit Don José Sepulvida.

He was at once seized and effusively embraced by the entire company with every protest of affection and respect. Not only Mr. Hamlin and Mr. Jenkinson, who accompanied him as invited guests, but Roberto in a new suit of clothes and guiltless of stain or trace of dissipation, shared in the pronounced friendliness of the kinsmen. Padre Felipe took snuff, Colonel Parker blew his nose gently.

Nor were they less demonstrative of their new convictions later at the banquet. Don José, with Jenkinson and the padre on his right and left, preserved his gentle and half-melancholy dignity in the midst of the noisy fraternisation. Even Padre Felipe, in a brief speech or exhortation proposing the health of their host, lent himself in his own tongue to this polite congeniality. 'We have had also, my friends and brothers,' he said in peroration, 'a pleasing example of the compliment of imitation shown by our beloved Don José. No one who has known him during his friendly sojourn in this community but will be struck with the conviction that he has acquired that most marvellous faculty of your great American nation, the exhibition of humour and of the practical joke.'

Every eye was turned upon the imperturbable face of Don José as he slowly rose to reply. 'In bidding you to this *fête*, my friends and kinsmen,' he began calmly, 'it was with the intention of formally embracing the habits, customs, and spirit of American institutions by certain methods of renunciation of the past, as became a *caballero* of honour and resolution. Those methods may possibly be known to some of you.' He paused for a moment as if to allow the members of his family to look unconscious. 'Since then, in the wisdom of God, it has occurred to me that my purpose may be as honourably effected by a discreet blending of the past and the present—in a word, by the judicious combination of the interests of my native people and the American nation. In consideration of that purpose, friends and kinsmen, I ask you to join me in drinking the good health of my host Señor Jenkinson, my future father-in-law, from whom I have to-day had the honour to demand the hand of the peerless Polly, his daughter, as the future mistress of the Rancho of the Blessed Innocents.'

The marriage took place shortly after. Nor was the free will and independence of Don José Sepulvida in the least opposed by his relations. Whether they felt they had already committed themselves, or had hopes in the future, did not transpire. Enough that the escapade of a week was tacitly forgotten. The only allusion ever made to the bridegroom's peculiarities was drawn from the demure lips of the bride herself on her installation at the 'Blessed Innocents.'

'And what, little one, didst thou find in me to admire?' Don José had asked tenderly.

'Oh, you seemed to be so much like that dear old Don Quixote, you know,' she answered demurely.

'Don Quixote,' repeated Don José with gentle gravity. 'But, my child, that was only a mere fiction—a romance, of one Cervantes. Believe me, of a truth there never was any such person!'

END OF VOL. I

'Good friends,' said Father Felipe, who had by this time recovered himself, taking out his snuff-box portentously, 'it would seem truly from the document which this discreet *caballero* has spoken of, that the errors of our dear Don José are rather of method than intent, and that while we may freely accept the one——'

'Pardon,' interrupted Colonel Parker with bland persistence, 'but I must point out to you that what we call in law "a consideration" is necessary to the legality of a conveyance, even though that consideration be frivolous and calculated to impair the validity of the document.'

'Truly,' returned the good padre insinuatingly, 'but if a discreet advocate were to suggest the substitution of some more pious and reasonable consideration——'

www.ingramcontent.com/pod-product-compliance
Lightning Source LLC
Chambersburg PA
CBHW020822230426
43666CB00007B/1057